IN THIS GUIDE

WITH THANKS

author's
acknowledgements

This travel series was conceived on a train between Budapest and Lake Balaton in Hungary. In trying to understand a place that was new and strange to me, my mind strayed to my home country, South Africa – to its magnificent diversity, its huge complexity, and the difficulties that visitors (and even local residents) might have in finding the right type of information and guidance for their travels. Fortunately, there are now a number of valuable guidebooks on South Africa, but these are mainly of a general nature and do not always provide the depth of insight that may be required by a traveller with a focused interest. The initial conception was a single book on 'alternative travel' in South Africa that would complement mainstream guides. However, it became apparent that a series of books would be more appropriate to the complexity of the task and to the diversity of interests that travellers have.

I have gained enormous personal satisfaction from putting these books together. Although the project has a serious intent, it has also been a wonderful hobby. It has provided a very good excuse for the travelling and exploration – activities that I have enjoyed since my early childhood years. In preparing the books, I have depended heavily on the inspiration, encouragement and practical assistance of many individuals. To begin, I am deeply indebted to my talented and highly organised research assistant, Monika Meyer-Prentice, and also to Stacey Sachs and Helena Saayman who did excellent work in researching the Western Cape and Eastern Cape. I am also grateful to Gustav Visser for his specialist input.

I owe a great debt of gratitude to my family and especially to my parents, John and Heather Harrison. Not only did they instil in me a love of travelling but they also provided enormous practical assistance in the production of this series. They spent long hours editing draft manuscripts, checking details with painstaking precision, and searching for and collating the photographs that illustrate these books. They did this at a time when I was out of the country and, without their on-site assistance, it would have been impossible to meet publishing deadlines. I also wish to express my deep and warm gratitude to other members of my large, extended family – my siblings and their partners – for their continued encouragement and help. In a real sense, this has been a family venture.

I have also been blessed with friends who provided the initial inspiration, ongoing support, practical assistance and, in some cases, much-appreciated company on my travels. Friends who have made a particular contribution to these books include Tracy Scott, Garth Klein, Brian Boshoff, Carolyn Frick, Shirley Brooks, Pauline Larsen, Sarah Charlton, Caroline Skinner, Paula Meth and Mzwanele Mayekiso. I am especially grateful to Heather Campbell for her affection and understanding during the process of producing this series.

MAKING CONTACT

For easy reference, **Making Contact** *directories listing the contact details of institutions, travel destinations and landmarks discussed on each page appear throughout this book. Be sure to make good use of them!*

south africa's top sites
ARTS & CULTURE

Philip Harrison

SPEARHEAD

An imprint of New Africa Books (Pty) Ltd
99 Garfield Road
Kenilworth
7700

(021) 674 4136

First edition, first impression 2005

ISBN 0-86486-565-1

Managing Editor Sean Fraser
Editor Peter Joyce
Design and typesetting Alida Kannemeyer, Fresh Identity
Cartography John Hall
Cover photograph National Arts Foundation
Photographic research John and Heather Harrison
Reproduction by House of Colours
Printed and bound by Paarl Print, Cape

PUBLISHER'S NOTE
Considerable care has been taken to ensure the accuracy of the
information in this guide. However, neither the publisher nor the
author can be held responsible for any liability that may arise from
the use of this information. Readers are advised that contact details
and other practical information provided herein tend to change
from time to time. Corrections, updated information and/or
additions may be sent to the Managing Editor, *Top Sites* Travel
Series, New Africa Books, PO Box 46963, Glosderry 7702.

It has also been a pleasure working with Spearhead Publishers and New Africa Books. They have always been supportive and have provided good management and constructive ideas, particularly Anita van Zyl, who helped get this project off the ground. I am especially grateful to the Managing Editor, Sean Fraser, and to Alida Kannemeyer for her design and typesetting. The publisher's editor, Peter Joyce, did an excellent job in improving and polishing the text, and has added considerable value to the writing. I enjoyed working with him. I am also grateful to Roelien Theron for providing detailed comments on early versions of the books, which were very useful in the final stages of writing.

Many other individuals and organisations have willingly provided information and photographs. It is, of course, not possible to name everyone individually, but I am nevertheless deeply grateful to them all. I do, however, wish to single out Haajirah Esau, District Six Museum Foundation; Michele Jacobs, Librarian at the School of Architecture at the University of KwaZulu-Natal; Santa van Bart, Groot Marico Information Centre; Ann Torlesse, Senior Curator at the National English Literary Museum; Professor Wium van Zyl, University of the Western Cape; Candi Nel, Johannesburg Art Gallery; Gillian Hemphill, National Arts Festival; Mark Wilby, The Owl House in Nieu Bethesda; Hannes de Beer, Oppikoppi Music Festival; Ann Pretorius, Director of the William Humphreys Art Gallery; and Glynnis Shewan of the Two Rivers Tourism Association. The photographs used in this book have been supplied by a number of valuable sources and I extend my thanks to them all.

Finally, this book is a celebration of the creative spirit that thrives within South Africa's diverse communities. Decades of political oppression failed to smother the imaginative energies of South Africa's people, and today this artistic exuberance is expressed in many forms, including in folklore, literature, music, dance, the visual arts and celebratory festivals.

PHILIP HARRISON

AND WHAT'S MORE...

To encourage readers to find out more about the initiatives and programmes discussed on these pages, these **And What's More...** panels provide further information on institutions and projects – via their websites, e-mail addresses and contact details.

THE WOW FACTOR!

For quick and easy reference, **The Wow Factor!** highlights the fascinating details and record-breaking statistics that help make South Africa such a remarkable travel destination.

INTRODUCTION

Art is so wonderfully irrational, exuberantly pointless,

but necessary all the same.

Nadine Gordimer

South Africa is a country of astonishing creativity, and it offers almost endless opportunities for the traveller interested in the arts. Perhaps this artistic richness has something to do with the country's traumatic past, but most certainly it has been stimulated, too, by the country's huge cultural diversity.

South African pictorial art goes back at least 77 000 years, to the time of the first known rock scratchings, and the country is famous for the prehistoric images that grace its cave walls and overhangs, but there is also a considerable and sometimes undervalued heritage of colonial and contemporary work. The painful years of apartheid provoked a moral anger that is reflected in, among other fields of activity, theatre and film, music and literature.

The arts, though, have expanded beyond political protest to address many other themes. The jazz and popular music of the townships is particularly vibrant. And there are many other musical genres. Given the relatively small size of the domestic market, South Africa's literary contribution is remarkable: a number of South African writers – among them Alan Paton, Nadine Gordimer and JM Coetzee – have achieved international acclaim. South African literature provides a compelling insight into the history of the country and the lives of its peoples. Architecture, too, also offers a window into South Africa's past, telling a story that ranges through the precolonial, colonial, apartheid, and post-apartheid eras.

Using this guide

This volume is aimed at all who are interested in the arts and literary heritage of South Africa. We begin by providing a window into the various fields, and then go on to describe, province by province, each of the top relevant venues.

Detailed directions are provided to only a few of the lesser-known sites, so this book should be used together with a good road atlas. We do, however, supply contact details – telephone numbers and, where available, websites. E-mail addresses are sometimes given, but bear in mind that most such addresses can be accessed through websites. Note too that this book does not usually give information on opening times for venues such as galleries and museums. The telephone numbers given are for domestic dialing; the international code for South Africa is 027, followed by the area code (dropping the zero) and the number.

READ ALL ABOUT IT!

For a day-to-day guide to events in the major urban centres, consult the following periodals, which boast up-to-date details on what's happening:
- *The Mail & Guardian*
- *Time Out*
- *SA City Life*
- *South African Country Life*
- *Sunday Times Lifestyle Magazine*
- *The Tonight!* sections in the daily newspapers of the *Independent Group*

Our choice!

Top Arts & Cultural Sites and Events

1. Rock-art sites across South Africa
2. Cape Town's Iziko museums
3. The Johannesburg Art Gallery (JAG)
4. The Newtown Cultural Precinct, Johannesburg
5. The National Arts Festival, Grahamstown
6. The Arts Alive Festival, Johannesburg
7. The Klein Karoo Nasionale Kunstefees, Oudtshoorn
8. The Joy of Jazz festivals
9. Sophiatown in Johannesburg
10. District Six in Cape Town
11. The Owl House at Nieu Bethesda
12. Cradock and its link with Olive Schreiner
13. Ixopo and its link with Alan Paton
14. Groot Marico and its link with Herman Charles Bosman
15. Jackson Hlungwani's New Jerusalem

ART IN AFRICA

THE VISUAL ARTS

The art of creating pictures goes back at least 77 000 years (the age of the rock engraving found in Blombos Cave on the southern Cape coast) and is represented by thousands of rock-art images scattered throughout the subcontinent. Large concentrations of actual *paintings* (as opposed to engravings) can be seen in the overhangs and caves of the Drakensberg-uKhahlamba mountains, the Cederberg mountains of the Western Cape, and the eastern highlands of the Free State. There are also significant accumulations of rock engravings in the Northern Cape.

Before the colonial era

It is hardly surprising, given the time span – nearly 80 000 years – and the vastness of the region, that different techniques and styles of rock art are represented. There are also different groups of artists, although it is widely believed that most engravings and paintings are attributable to the San (Bushman) and their immediate ancestors.

Pigments were ground from iron oxides, clays, bone and plants; they were mixed with water, blood, urine, and vegetable juices, and applied with the hairs of an antelope's tail, or the finger or palm of the hand. Many paintings are monochrome (single colour), but others are polychrome (multicoloured) images, and represent a degree of artistic sophistication. There are also different types, some involving fine lines cut into the rock's patina (skin), others the scratching or even removal of the patina.

The big rock-art debate

The subjects of paintings and engravings are varied. Animals and human figures are common, but there are also mysterious images, including creatures that appear to be part-human, part-animal. In places such as Driekopseiland in the Northern Cape, images are highly abstract, with concentric and spiral shapes, cross-hatching, and other geometric forms.

Rock art is the subject of much speculation. The most significant work has come from David Lewis-Williams and his colleagues at the Rock Art Institute at the University of the Witwatersrand, who have argued that the art has to be understood in terms of the San's beliefs and practices. For more on these debates, see the companion volumes *Science* and *Spiritual* in *South Africa's Top Sites* series.

Iron Age arts and crafts

The Iron Age communities of South Africa were also talented in bead-work, basketry, pottery, and carving. Among the remarkable examples of precolonial art are the **Lydenburg Heads**, seven terracotta masks that may date back 1 500 years. These are on display at the South African Museum in Cape Town. See also *South Africa's Top Sites – Science*.

Zulu, Xhosa and Ndebele women were skilled at beadwork, producing necklaces, bracelets and ornaments rich in symbolism. Important among the Zulu and Sotho was woodcarving, and murals among the Ndebele.

Cultural villages

These 'living museums' have become increasingly popular tourist stops, especially among international travellers. Many have been criticised for their commercialism, and for presenting its elements as static, locked into traditional frameworks, but they do offer access to at least something of the region's heritage – and provide local communities with much-needed income.

The colonial period

Until the late 19th century, colonial art was mainly about recording the landscapes of southern Africa for those living in the 'mother countries'. The work of **Thomas Baines** is an excellent example of this 'realism'.

By the end of that century, however, there was some attempt to develop a specifically South African approach to art, a shift that is evident, for example, in the paintings of **Hugo Naudé**, and the sculpture of **Anton van Wouw**. As Shaun de Waal wrote, 'their work is the first glimpse of an artistic vision engaging with life as lived in South Africa, for its own sake, rather than as a "report" to the colonial master'. Naude, who was South Africa's first professional artist, was a pioneer impressionist, while Van Wouw's work focused on human emotion rather than landscape.

This shift was even more pronounced by the early 20th century. **JH Pierneef**, whose work was to inspire Afrikaner nationalists, used geometric forms to depict the landscape, while **Irma Stern**, South Africa's leading female painter, produced bold, subjective art under the influence of German Expressionism. She studied in Germany but spent time in Italy and the south of France.

AND WHAT'S MORE...

Irma Stern was born in the small town of Schweizer-Reneke in what was then the Transvaal in 1894, but spent her formative years in Germany where she had formal training in art. She was, however, also strongly influenced by visits to Zanzibar and the Congo, and her art represents both the influence of German Expressionists and the vivid interpretations of African traditional work. For more information, visit the website www.irmastern.co.za or contact the **Irma Stern Museum** *in Cape Town on (021) 685 5686.*

art in africa

Post-war impetus

The First World War (1914–18) was an important catalyst for the development of art in South Africa. Returning soldiers and post-war immigrants from Europe exposed local artists to a diversity of new styles and techniques. **Maurice van Essche**, for example, brought Modernist techniques from Belgium but linked these to South African subject matter, while the sculptor **Edoardo Villa** displayed a distinctively Italian influence. He came to South Africa as a prisoner-of-war but decided to stay on.

Artists such as **Alexis Preller** and **Cecil Skotnes** connected European Modernism with the African idiom, producing a local style that Marilyn Martin described as 'technically European but iconographically African'. Preller, for example, was strongly influenced by the work of Van Gogh and Gauguin but also fascinated by the African mystique. Perhaps the most important post-war artist was **Walter Battiss**, whose work was powerfully influenced by the content and technique of South Africa's rock art.

Although white South African artists were inspired by African themes, they were to be criticised for their lack of engagement with the realities of political oppression and racial discrimination in South Africa.

The black artists

In the early days black South Africans generally lacked resources to work as artists and were largely excluded from the mainstream art community. However, by the first half of the 20th century, urbanisation had brought a new generation of talented individuals to the city, men and women who were able to connect with European artistic traditions while still drawing on the African world for inspiration. **Gerard Sekoto**, for example, captured the vibrancy of District Six and Sophiatown; **George Pemba** painted life in his home township of Motherwell, Port Elizabeth; **Ernest Mancoba** challenged racial conventions with his famous *Black Madonna* sculpture. Many other black artists were to follow the path blazed by these pioneers.

The apartheid years

Edoardo Villa was born in Italy in 1920. His first experience of South Africa was as a prisoner-of-war but, undaunted, he stayed on, and was to emerge as South Africa's leading sculptor, representing the country five times at the Vienna Biennale. The **Edoardo Villa Museum**, *now located at the University of Pretoria, may be contacted on (012) 420 4017.*

Racial segregation had a double-edged effect on art in South Africa. On one hand it was deeply repressive, and South Africa lost a lot of talent as artists either left the country or succumbed to the dead weight of a bigoted and censorious regime. On the other hand, however, resistance to the system unlocked creative energy, inspiring intense and lively art.

By the 1980s resistance art was the major genre. One of the most acclaimed artists of this period was **William Kentridge**, who used highly personalised metaphors to depict a tortured country in a state of siege. Kentridge remains South Africa's leading artist, and is highly regarded internationally (*see page 86*). The sculptor **Jane Alexander** achieved considerable acclaim with her skulking *Butcher Boys* (*see* Cape Town's National Art Gallery *on page 28*) which, like her other works, explores themes of aggression, violence, power, and subservience. Equally bleak and challenging was **Paul Stopforth's** *Struggle Art* with its focus on torture. **Penny Siopis** provided a different angle on the Struggle with her forceful representations of the history of slaves, women and children in colonial society.

Increasingly, too, black artists used their talents to express their anger at the injustice in South African society. The new generation of black artists included **Seoka Phutuma, Eric Ngcobo, Michael Zondi, Selby Mvusi, David Mogano, David Koloane, Sydney Khumalo** and **Noria Mabasa**.

Two institutions, in particular, were instrumental in providing support to economically disadvantaged black artists. The first was the **Polly Street Art Centre** (later the Jubilee Art Centre) in Johannesburg, established and run by **Cecil Skotnes**, the second the **Rorke's Drift Mission** in rural KwaZulu-Natal, which supported a new generation of artists from very poor rural areas. Later, other community art centres – including FUBA and FUNDA in Soweto and the African Cultural Centre in Newtown, Johannesburg – nurtured many of the black artists who were to enter the mainstream and challenge the supremacy of South Africa's historically advantaged white artists.

While these white and black artists engaged vigorously with social and political themes, another group responded to the pressures of life by retreating into a private world and producing work that defied any accepted convention. These were 'outsider artists' such as **Helen Martins** of Nieu Bethesda, who created a bizarre fantasy world of concrete statues, mirrors, and crushed glass; **Jackson Hlungwani** from a small village in Limpopo, who built a hilltop citadel with mythical and religious sculptures after experiencing a religious vision; and **Nukain Mabasa**, who painted elaborate designs on the hillside near Revolver Creek in Mpumalanga.

Art through the lens

From the 1960s photography matured as an art form in South Africa, and made its contribution to political resistance in South Africa. One of the country's leading photographers is **David Goldblatt**, who achieved considerable international acclaim. **Peter Magubane** is the other giant of South African photography: he has recorded the traumas and wonders of South African life for almost 50 years, working as a photojournalist in South Africa for *Bantu World* and *Drum* and in New York for *Time Magazine*. His books include the beautifully illustrated *Vanishing Cultures*. Major contributions have also been made by, among others, Eli Weinberg, Paul Weinberg, David Southwood, Hannelie Coetzee, Ken Oosterbroek, and Greg Marinovich.

The age of freedom

The past decade or so has been both a difficult and exciting time for the visual arts in South Africa. Difficult in that the exhilaration and energy of struggle and protest has ended, but exciting for the opportunities it provides to reconnect with the rest of the world. From the early 1990s, for the first time in many years, South African artists were invited to international events, and at least a trickle of internationally known individuals have made their way to South Africa. The first Johannesburg Biennale (1995), for example, provided an opportunity to show the world what South Africa had to offer.

READ ALL ABOUT IT!

THE VISUAL ARTS
• Rayda Becker and Rochelle Keene, Art Routes: A Guide to South African Art Collections *(Witwaters-rand University Press)*
• Philippa Dissel, The Zebra Register of South African Artists and Galleries *(Dissel Marketing and Research)*
• Anne Emslie, The Owl House *(Viking)*
• David Lewis-Williams and Geoffrey Blundell, Fragile Heritage: A Rock Art Field Guide *(Witwatersrand University Press)*
• Mike van Graan and Tammy Ballantyne, The South African Handbook on Arts & Culture *(David Philip Publishers)*

This period has also been one of innovation in terms of the form and style. We have seen, for example, the emergence of a 'conceptual art' that brings painting together with the use of other mediums such as sculpture, photography, video, performance, and the use of earth materials. Artists who are pushing the boundaries of what is considered to be visual art include Sue Williamson, Jeremy Wafer, Sandile Zulu, Marc Edwards, Steven Cohen, and Kendell Geers. There has also been a revival of traditional crafts, and the blurring of the distinctions between high art and folk art. Today, crafts can be seen together with the paintings of South Africa's leading artists in the top art galleries of the country as well as in the myriad craft markets around the country.

STAGE AND SCREEN

South African theatre has struggled to establish an indigenous identity. The first formal production, it's believed, was the1838 performance of **Andrew Geddes Bain**'s *Kaatje Kekkelbek* (or *Life Amongst the Hottentots*) by the Graham's Town Amateur Company. Within the black African community the productions by **Father Bernard Hess** of the Mariannhill mission near Durban in the 1920s proved to be formative and inspirational. A key figure in emergent African theatre was KwaZulu-Natal's **Herbert Dhlomo**, whose 1935 production, *The Girl Who Killed to Save*, was the first play by a black South African written in English.

Theatre became increasingly popular in the townships through the 1940s and 1950s. In 1959 the creativity in these disadvantaged areas, and especially in the Johannesburg suburb of **Sophiatown**, exploded onto the international scene with the sensational musical *King Kong*, which was first performed in the Great Hall of the University of the Witwatersrand before a multiracial audience. In later years *District Six – the Musical*, created by the Western Cape's **David Kramer** and **Taliep Petersen**, was also to inspire productions that achieved international acclaim.

It was in the late 1950s that **Athol Fugard**, a playwright from Port Elizabeth, made his first appearance on the scene. Fugard was to become the colossus of local theatre, a champion of the Struggle. His plays include *The Blood Knot, Hello and Goodbye, Boesman and Lena, 'Master Harold'… and the Boys!*, and *The Road to Mecca*.

Emergent theatre

The township theatre movement grew apace through the 1960s and 1970s, despite the lack of infrastructure and facilities.

Politicisation and the emergence of the Black Consciousness movement in the 1970s was a powerful stimulus to creative talent, inspiring the work of, among others, **Zakes Mda**, whose plays included *Dead End* (1973) and *We Shall Sing for the Fatherland* (1973). There was a desperate need for venues that would support this emergent work and, in the 1970s, experimental venues appeared, among them the Space Theatre and Baxter Theatre in Cape Town and, most importantly, the establishment of the **Market Theatre** in Newtown, Johannesburg, where Fugard, Mda, Gibson Kente, Adam Small, Percy Mtwa, Mbongeni Ngema and many others played to multiracial audiences in defiance of authority.

THE WOW FACTOR!

In 1929 a student at the Pietersburg Christian School, **Ernest Mancoba**, *caused a scandal when he sculpted a figure of the Madonna – the Virgin Mary – with negroid features. Mancoba left for Europe in the 1930s, where he founded the Cobra Group of artists. He returned to South Africa in 1994, and died in 2002 at the age of 98. The famous* **Black Madonna** *was displayed in St Mary's Cathedral, Johannesburg, before being placed in the Johannesburg Art Gallery. Following Mancoba, many other black Madonnas have been sculpted and painted, including the famous painting in the Regina Mundi Church, Soweto.*

The Market, indeed, was the fount of resistance theatre in South Africa. One of the finest performances of all times was *Woza Albert!* (1981), produced as a collaboration between Percy Mtwa, Mbongeni Ngema and the artistic director of the Market Theatre, Barney Simon. This magnificent piece of protest art contrasts dramatically with another popular musical of the time, *Ipi Tombi*, which played into the stereotypes of traditional black society. *Woza Albert!* was followed by Ngema's *Asinimali* (1985) and his hit musical *Sarafina!* (1986), a musical play based on the Soweto uprising of 1976.

Coming to prominence in the 1980s was the political satirist, **Pieter-Dirk Uys**, who lampooned the leaders of the apartheid state with his biting humour. This Struggle theatre provided a vital alternative to the state-sponsored productions supported by the National Theatre Organisation until 1963, and thereafter by the Performing Arts Councils.

The new breed
With the ending of apartheid, and the need for resistance, much of the spirit that inspired the arts in the '80s was gone, and community theatre, in particular, struggled to survive. Recently, however, there has been a partial revival. In Johannesburg's **Newtown**, at **Artscape** in Cape Town, and elsewhere, new playwrights and actors are emerging, men and women who are dealing courageously with themes such as HIV/Aids, gay and lesbian life, the empowerment of women, violence, and personal relationships – concerns that were, perhaps, never given prominence during the heady days of political struggle. South Africa has also contributed to the performing arts internationally. One of the United Kingdom's top Shakespearean actors, **Antony Sher**, was born in the Little Karoo settlement of Middelpos and raised and educated in Cape Town.

The silver screen
South Africa's film industry was launched early in the 20th century. A weekly cinema newsreel appeared in 1913, and three years later media magnate IW Schlesinger founded Killarney Studios. Within six years Killarney had produced 43 films, among them *De Voortrekkers*, a sentimental feature-length account of the Great Trek. But a flood of international movies was to depress the industry from the early 1920s, and it was only in the '50s that significant investment returned to the local film world.

During much of the apartheid era, South African film remained undistinguished, serving as propaganda for the regime. About two-thirds of the films produced under the subsidy were in Afrikaans and geared to a small domestic market, making virtually no international impact.

By the 1970s a very particular movie genre had emerged. The 'border film' romanticised the South African Defence Force's war in Namibia and Angola. In the 1980s the incentive structure allowed the shifting of money offshore, ostensibly to make films but essentially as a ploy to counteract international sanctions and some very poor-quality productions were released (although there were exceptions, notably the Jamie Uys comedy, *The Gods Must be Crazy*, followed in later years by Leon Schuster's *There's a Zulu on My Stoep*, *Millenium Menace* and *Mr Bones*).

art in africa

Films on the fringe

While state-sponsored features dominated the domestic scene throughout the apartheid era, there were nevertheless some courageous attempts to provide alternative cinema. In 1951, for example, Zoltan Zorba produced a filmed version of Alan Paton's *Cry, The Beloved Country.*

From the late 1970s fringe films did confront the apartheid system, but they were constrained by small budgets and the threat of censorship. By the end of the 1980s, however, there were significant breakthroughs in alternative cinema. Major films included Anant Singh and Darrell Roodt's *Place of Weeping*; Oliver Schmidt's township melodrama, *Mapantsula*; Katinka Heyns' *Paljas*, and Anant Singh's filming of Mbongeni Ngema's *Sarafina*. From the mid-'80s alternative expositions, notably the *Weekly Mail's* festival, provided an important outlet for independent productions.

Film has moved on from its '80s focus on political protest to addressing a range of other concerns, including crime, and gay and lesbian issues. Important full-length productions have included *Hijack Stories*, a view of Soweto through the eyes of a gangster; *Stander*, the story of a notorious bank robber; and *Proteus*, a sensitive account of gay love on Robben Island. There has also been a strong focus on short films, through international initiatives such as 'African Dreaming', which provide a stage for new producers lacking the resources to film full-length features. An excellent example of a short film is Ntshaveni wa Luruli's *Chikin Biznis*.

South African film has also been promoted through collective shows such as the Out in Africa gay and lesbian film festival, which is hosted by the Cinema Nouveau theatres in Cape Town, Johannesburg and Durban. Over the past decade South Africa has emerged as a major international location for film-making. By 2003 there were over 50 production houses in Cape Town alone.

SOUNDS OF MUSIC

Popular music in South Africa has deep roots – the rhythmic drumming of the San (Bushman) and the traditional melodies of the black peoples have greatly influenced its development, the indigenous forms fusing with European and American styles.

The evolution of music took interesting and different turns in different regions of the country. In the **Western Cape**, for example, the Malay slaves combined Dutch and Khoekhoen folksongs with the spirituals of occasional African-American visitors to produce the so-called *ghoemaliedjies* (the half-Dutch, half-Malay ditties), which were initially a form of satire performed by slaves and directed against their white masters. From the 1820s onwards, on the day after New Year, the streets of Cape Town echoed with the colourful *ghoemaliedjies* of what was then referred to as the 'Coon Carnival' but is now called the Cape Minstrel Carnival.

Missionaries exerted a powerful influence in the **Eastern Cape**, the traditional Xhosa harmonic patterns blending with Christian hymns to produce the compelling harmonies of South African gospel. The most famous of indigenous hymns of the region was *Nkosi Sikelel' iAfrika*, composed by Enoch Sontonga in 1897. Much later, the hymn was to become half of the hybrid post-liberation national anthem.

In **KwaZulu-Natal**, there was a similar fusion as traditional and spiritual music developed into a vocal style with rich harmonies known as *cappella*, most famously rendered in Linda Solomon's 1939 song *Mbube*, basis of Disney's theme song, *The Lion Sleeps Tonight*. Cappella was to evolve into a style known as *iscathamiya* (meaning to 'stalk' or 'step softly'), which was brought to international attention by Ladysmith Black Mambazo.

The orchestral scene

In the early years of the last century symphony orchestras were formed in Johannesburg, Cape Town and Durban, together with a National Symphony Orchestra sponsored for many decades by the South African Broadcasting Corporation (SABC). South African composers and classical performers achieved some international success. **Mimi Coertse**, for example, was widely acclaimed in Austria, Germany and elsewhere from the 1950s; the South African composer **Kevin Voland's** quartet, Pieces of Africa, topped the US Classical and World Music charts for 26 weeks.

After 1994, however, the orchestras came under pressure as classical music was widely perceived to be a white, elitist art form, and a lot of effort was invested in transforming the scene with outreach and educational programmes, and through support for economically disadvantaged black performers (some of whom, such as Sibongile Mngoma and Virginia Davids, have achieved considerable success). However, this was not enough to protect the orchestras from huge cutbacks in funding, and in 2000 the National Symphony Orchestra collapsed when the SABC withdrew its sponsorship. Later, the orchestras in Cape Town and Durban also closed.

For a while it seemed that South Africa's classical music tradition, which was so dependent on public monies, would die. However, there was a regrouping. The 70-piece **KwaZulu-Natal Philharmonic** (originally the Natal Philharmonic), which had been founded in 1983, survived and consolidated its position as the country's (and Africa's) leading orchestra, and is continuing to expand under the leadership of its black African director, Bongani Tembe. It performs for the most part in the Durban City Hall, but also uses other venues, among them Durban Botanical Gardens. Members of the defunct Durban Philharmonic eventually regrouped as the **Gateway Philharmonic Orchestra** but, at the time of writing, it finding it difficult to secure sponsorship and its future was uncertain.

In Johannesburg, some members of the defunct National Symphony Orchestra reconstituted themselves as the Johannesburg Philharmonic, which employs musicians on a freelance basis and gives performances in the Johannesburg Civic Theatre and elsewhere. Musicians from Cape Town Philharmonic regrouped as the **Cape Philharmonic Orchestra**, which operates on a similar basis to its Johannesburg counterpart, and can be heard mainly at the Artscape complex on the Foreshore area of Cape Town. There's also the **Eastern Cape Philharmonic** in Port Elizabeth; a small, professional **Chamber Orchestra of South Africa** (COSA) at the University of Pretoria, and a number of youth orchestras.

Despite the severe challenges it has faced in recent years, the classical music tradition in South Africa has shown both resilience and also a capacity to transform.

READ ALL ABOUT IT!

MUSIC
• Rob Allingham, 'Popular Music: The voice of the nation', World Music: The Rough Guide *(Penguin)*
• Rob Allingham, 'South African Jazz: Hip kings, hip queens', World Music: The Rough Guide *(Penguin)*
• Christopher Ballantine, Marabi Nights: Early South African Jazz and Vaudeville *(Ravan Press)*
• David Coplan, In Township Tonight: South Africa's Black City Music and Theatre *(Ravan Press)*
• Mike Nicol, A Good-Looking Corpse: The World of Drum – Jazz and Gangsters, Hope and Defiance in the Townships of South Africa *(Secker & Warburg)*

Township music

It was, however, the slums and townships of the rapidly urbanising mining and industrial centres of the **Witwatersrand** (Gauteng) that produced the most striking musical innovations. The first of the new styles was *marabi*, which combined traditional music forms with American dixieland and ragtime. It had enticing rhythm and melody, and was initially used simply to draw people into the shebeens – the illegal taverns – of the township, but was later to evolve into a sophisticated swing-jazz known as *mbaqanga*.

The other ingredient in the mix was *kwela*, which came to the Witwatersrand in the 1940s with the humble pennywhistle – derived from the traditional reed flute of rural cattle-herders. In the 1940s and 1950s small groups of pennywhistlers roamed the townships, and later the white suburbs (where they engaged in a cat-and-mouse game with the police). In the 1960s, the pennywhistle was replaced by the saxophone to produce the sax jives of *mbaqanga* of groups such as the Dark City Sisters, the Mahotella Queens and Abafana Baseqhudeni. A major factor in the development of *mbaqanga* and other South African music was the birth of South Africa's recording industry in the 1930s, when Eric Gallo set up Gallo Records.

While this popular music was evolving, a more sophisticated sound emerged from the most vibrant and cosmopolitan of all the urban slums, **Sophiatown**. The new city-dwellers here reacted to the traditionalism of rural South Africa by looking to the sophisticated lifestyles and music of Black America as their model. They brought together the township music of their own country and post-war American bebop jazz to create a distinctively South African swing-jazz, most brilliantly represented perhaps in the hit musical *King Kong* (1959). It is this music, which had its roots in the anxieties of urban Africans, that is most closely associated with South Africa's painful and turbulent history. As Christopher Ballantine explained in his book *Marabi Nights*, it was a form of both comfort and protest, and, in addition, a means for maginalised black South Africans to achieve recognition on the world stage.

The jazz scene

The jazz clubs of the 1950s spawned a veritable array of stars – Kippies Moeketsi, Dolly Rathebe, Miriam Makeba, Chris MacGregor, Ntemi Piliso, Jonas Gwangwa, Hugh Masekela and, most importantly, **Abdullah Ibrahim** (initially known as Dollar Brand). The bands that played on the concert and dance circuit of the time included the African Swingsters, the Manhattan Brothers, the Skylarks, the Mahotella Queens, and the all-time great, the **African Jazz Pioneers**, who recorded South Africa's first jazz album.

Many of this generation were forced into exile during the 1960s – following the police clampdown after the Sharpeville massacre – and returned only in the 1990s. After 1964 the vibrancy of South African jazz was greatly diminished and, in the absence of its leading exponents, the 1970s and 1980s were a period of steep decline.

Although exile undoubtedly had a negative effect on local music, it did serve the purpose of bringing South African jazz to an international

THE WOW FACTOR!

As a child, Adolphe Johannes Brand was nick-named 'Dollar' because he was always carrying money to buy jazz albums from American sailors. In the late 1960s, sometime after he formed the famous Jazz Epsitles with Hugh Masekela, he converted to Islam and changed his name to **Abdullah Ibrahim***.*

audience. Hugh Masekela, Abdullah Ibrahim and Miriam Makeba, in particular, attained enormous international acclaim and secured for South Africa its reputation as one of the world's leading centres of creative jazz.

Nevertheless, there were a few individuals and bands that kept the jazz tradition alive within the country during these dark years, including, most importantly, **Philip Tabane** and the African Jazz Pioneers. And, since the coming of full democracy in 1994 and the return of the greats, South African jazz has experienced something of a revival. The first-generation artists are now being supported by a new breed that includes Jimmy Dludlu, Sipho Gumede, Don Laka and Gloria Bosman, and popular bands such as Tananas. Sadly, one of the famous Tananas trio, **Gito Baloi**, was shot dead in downtown Johannesburg in April 2004.

The major sponsor of jazz in South Africa is Standard Bank, which contributes through its **Joy of Jazz** festivals. While jazz experienced its ups and downs, popular music continued to evolve. From KwaZulu-Natal came *Iscathamiya* (the compelling fusion of traditional music and spirituals) and achieved a national following – and then an international reputation through Joseph Shabalala's band **Ladysmith Black Mambazo**: the band's 1973 *Amabutho* was the first album in Africa to achieve Gold Record status. Then, in 1986, superstar Paul Simon discovered the rich harmonies of *Iscathamiya* and collaborated with Shabalala and his group to produce one of the best-selling recordings ever – *Graceland*. Since then Ladysmith Black Mambazo has released more than 30 gold albums. In the 1970s, too, Sipho Mchunu and the 'white Zulu', Johnny Clegg, established the remarkable partnership known as **Juluka** (renamed Savuka), which combined Zulu traditional music with Western rock. Also with traditional roots, and playing on the international circuit, are the contemporary bands Amapondo and Urban Creep.

Soul, bubblegum and kwaito

In the late 1960s American Soul became popular in the townships, and local versions of the genre, with an added touch of 1970s disco music, began to be heard. Bands included the Movers, Soul Brothers and the Cannibals (later Stimela). Artists such as Ray Phiri and Sipho 'Hotstix' Mabuse achieved a huge following in the 1970s and the early to mid-1980s by mixing Western pop with American soul and traditional rhythms. In due course soul had evolved into a light dance pop, popularly known as 'bubblegum', which combined catchy melodies and lyrics with electronic gadgetry. One of the first great bubblegum hits was **Yvonne Chaka Chaka's** *I'm in love with a DJ* (1984).

Yvonne Chaka Chaka became immensely popular throughout Africa, and today rivals Ladysmith Black Mambazo as South Africa's greatest commercial success. Her main rival was **Brenda Fassie**, popularly known as Africa's 'queen of pop' and the 'girl with the golden voice', whose top albums each had sales of more than 500 000. Fassie, however, struggled with problems of alcoholism and drug addiction, and died tragically in 2004 at the age of 40. It was also in the 1980s that **reggae** arrived in South Africa. Bob Marley became popular in the townships; South African **Lucky Dube** emerged as one of Africa's top reggae artists.

AND WHAT'S MORE...

While jazz indeed has a wide and diverse following worldwide, it enjoys a special place in the hearts of South African music lovers. There are a number of festivals celebrating the genre locally, most notably the North Sea Jazz Festival (now officially known as the **Cape Town International Jazz Festival** *– book through Computicket 083 915 8000 or via the website nsjfcapetown.com) and Standard Bank's* **Joy of Jazz** *festivals, www.joyofjazz.co.za*

art in africa

By the late 1990s a new genre had captured the hearts of the township youth. Known as **kwaito** (named after the *Amakwaito* gangsters), this form of music combined American-style rap and hip-hop with local form. It is an electronically generated sound associated with a rythmic pelvic dance known as 'slow jam'. *Kwaito*, linked with musicians such as Boom Shaka, Bongo Maffin and M'du, has been referred to as South Africa's first post-apartheid music genre, but the older generation, who have memories of the township music of the 1950s, have condemned it as a frivolous form of techno/hip-hop.

White idols

Meanwhile, most white South Africans were listening to European-style music, others to the traditional Afrikaner sounds of what is known as **boeremusiek**, which is similar to American Country.

By the 1980s a handful of white South African rock and pop groups had achieved a level of international recognition, among them **Four Jacks and a Jill** (which successfully toured the US, UK and Australia) and teen sensation **Rabbitt**.

Punk, the music of a rebellious youth, had arrived in South Africa by the late 1970s and flourished in white working-class areas such as the East Rand and in sultry Durban. The anti-establishment spirit of this form of music fed into the emergence of an alternative **Afrikaner rock culture** which, by the mid 1980s, was provocatively challenging the Calvinist norms of mainstream Afrikanerdom. The key figures in this movement were Johannes Kerkorrel (and his Gereformeerde Blues Band), Koos Kombuis, Bernoldus Niemand (or James Philips) and Anton Goosen, who composed the first ever Afrikaans rock song in 1979 ('Blommetjie Gedenk aan My'). They provided an alternative to the more mainstream Afrikaner singers such as Sonja Herholdt and Carike Keuzenkamp.

Current (2004) pop idols among Afrikaner youth include Steve Hofmeyr and Karen Zoid; the most successful contemporary rock band was **Springbok Nude Girls**. Pop and rock remain primarily the music of white youth, and the small size of the market makes it difficult for local bands to survive. There is, however, a degree of crossover between black and white genres, which was evident, for example, in the music of popular contemporary group such as Mango Groove and eVoid.

EVENTS

South Africa is a country of festivals. Three decades ago they were very small, local affairs, but the launch of the Grahamstown Festival in 1974 prompted a new and grander approach. At first Grahamstown attracted just a few hundred enthusiasts, but it grew exponentially to peak at more than 100 000. Initially it celebrated English culture in South Africa – strongly associated with the legacy of the 1820 British settlers – but eventually shifted towards a more inclusive programme and was eventually renamed the **National Festival of the Arts**.

The status of the Grahamstown occasion as South Africa's premier cultural celebration was eventually to be challenged. In 1991, the **Arts Alive Festival** was launched in Johannesburg, and was soon attracting tens of thousands to its main events, among them the popular Jazz on the Lake concert. By the late 1990s all other major urban centres had launched their own festivals – the **Cape Town Festival** (known initially as the One City Festival); **Awesome Africa** in Durban; and, **Macufe** in Bloemfontein. All these celebrated a new and widely defined South Africanism.

The Afrikaner community responded to the predominance of the English language in the various cultural celebrations by organising their own events. The **Klein Karoo Nasionale Kunstefees** (KKNK) began life in 1995, in the town of Oudtshoorn, as the Afrikaner's alternative to Grahamstown and was soon attracting more than 100 000 visitors. This was followed three years later by the launch of the **Aardklop Nasionale Kunstefees** in Potchefstroom. These mainly Afrikaans occasions, however, have also shifted in recent years to become more inclusive.

These large 'national' festivals are complemented by a number of smaller ones that focus almost solely on music. Leading the way was **Splashy Fen**, which started in 1990 on a farm near Underberg in the foothills of KwaZulu-Natal's Drakensberg mountains. Gauteng now has the Woodstock and Womad festivals, while Standard Bank supports a series of jazz jamborees across the country, the largest of which is Cape Town's highly acclaimed **North Sea Jazz Festival**.

Many other **specialist festivals** have emerged in recent years, taking in film (for example, the Apollo exposition, held in the Little Karoo town of Victoria West); women interests; poetry and writing (for instance, the Urban Voices International Arts Festival), and the gay and lesbian community (notably the Pink Loerie Festival in Knysna and the Out in Africa Film Festival in Cape Town, Johannesburg, and Durban).

THE PRINTED WORD

African oral traditions are profoundly important but have been largely ignored in the telling of the story of South African literature. Indeed they are in danger of being lost altogether.

However, a few writers, most notably **Cyril Nyembezi**, author of *Zulu Proverbs* (1954), and African 'high priest' **Credo Mutwa**, have attempted to record the folk tales of the African people. The controversial 'people's poet' **Mzwakhe Mbuli** has also continued the oral tradition.

The arrival of European settlers in 1652 introduced the written word to the region, but it took a long while for any form of South African literature to emerge. The earliest writings were the travelogues of adventurers and explorers, whose work was intended to describe an exotic continent for an audience back in Europe. Among the more notable of such writers (and poets) were William Burchell, Thomas Pringle, David Livingstone, and Andrew Geddes Bain. There were also the charming diaries of Lady Anne Barnard, which provide an intriguing and perceptive insight into life in the Cape Colony at the end of the 18th century. Probably the best of these early authors was **Thomas Pringle**, who used his poetry to protest the treatment of the African peoples and who showed a true respect for African tradition, even if his work was still framed by the images of colonialism.

AND WHAT'S MORE...

For the Woodstock experience, find your way to **Splashy Fen** *music festival on a farm in the foothills of KwaZulu-Natal's southern Drakensberg. The festival has been running for more than 15 years and is one of South Africa's most important music events. Visit the website www.splashyfen.co.za*

Schreiner and others

The major catalyst for the true advent of English literature in South Africa was the arrival of 4 000 British settlers on the eastern frontier of the Cape Colony in the 1820s. The first internationally acclaimed 19th-century South African novel was **Olive Schreiner's** *The Story of an African Farm* (1883), which has been favourably compared with Emily Brontë's *Wuthering Heights*.

Schreiner's novel was firmly set within the English liberal tradition, and brought a deep appreciation of the Karoo landscape together with an evocative account of a personal search for fulfilment and meaning within a colonial situation. The liberal humanitarian tradition – associated with the writings of Thomas Pringle and Olive Schreiner in the Cape, and with John and Harriet Colenso in Natal – was, however, to be eclipsed at the end of the century by a literature rooted in colonial fantasies.

A romanticised Victorian image of an Africa of noble savages, deep mysteries and hidden wealth underlies the work of writers such as **H Rider Haggard** (*King Solomon's Mines*, 1885; *Alan Quatermain*, 1887; *She*, 1887, and *Nada the Lily*,1892), **Percy Fitzpatrick** (*Jock of the Bushveld*, 1907), and **John Buchan** (*Prester John*, 1910). This literary genre is echoed in the contemporary popular writings of **Wilbur Smith**, who offers a recipe of big-game safaris and adult sex in an exotic Africa.

Challenges to the colonial mindset

In the first half of the 20th century, South Africa's leading novelist was **Sarah Gertrude Millin**, though her reputation has suffered greatly in recent times as her race-obsessed works reflect the deep colour prejudices of colonial society. In *God's Stepchildren* (1924), for example, Millin recounted a story of how interracial sex led to fatal genetic flaws in subsequent generations.

In the 1926, however, colonial society was challenged and provoked by the publication of a very different sort of book – **William Plomer's** *Turbott Wolfe* (written when he was just 19 years old) provided a highly sensitive account of love across the colour line. The young Plomer was to join **Laurens van der Post** and **Roy Campbell** in producing the literary journal *Voorslag* (meaning 'Whiplash'), which confronted what they believed to be the philistinism of South African colonial society. All three writers were to leave South Africa and establish international reputations, insisting that South Africa could never really appreciate their genius. Van der Post, the romantic mystic, was to become the godfather and mentor of Prince Charles; Roy Campbell, who had established his reputation with the *The Flaming Terrapin* in 1924, became one of the more respected of 20th-century poets, although his reputation was sullied by his support for facism during the 1930s, and he attracted controversy with his attack on the Bloomsbury (London) literary group.

Cultures crossed

The other major early 20th-century literary genre was the tale of rural community life (known in Afrikaans as the *plaasroman*). In English its two leading exponents were **Pauline Smith** and **Herman Charles Bosman**.

READ ALL ABOUT IT!

• Peter Alexander, Alan Paton: A Biography (Oxford University Press)
• Michael Chapman (Ed.), A Century of South African Poetry (AD Donker)
• Michael Chapman, Southern African Literatures (University of Natal Press)
• Tim Couzens and Essop Patel, The Return of the Amasi Bird (Ravan Press)
• Heidi Holland and Adam Roberts (Eds), From Jo'burg to Jozi: Stories about South Africa's Infamous City (Penguin)
• D Ricci, Reef of Time: Johannesburg in Writing (AD Donker)

Both authors wrote in English about Afrikaner life. Smith grew up in the Little Karoo, near Oudtshoorn, and came to know many isolated country folk when joining her father, a medical doctor, on his visits to Afrikaner farming families. Her impressions were captured in *The Beadle* (1926) and *Platkops Children* (1935).

Herman Charles Bosman taught briefly in a rural Afrikaans-medium school in the remote district of Groot Marico (*see also pages 116–117*). His observations of characters in this remote community provided material for the many humorous and gently ironic stories in such collections as *Mafeking Road* (1947), *Unto Dust* (1949) and *A Cask of Jerepigo* (1957).

Troubled consciences

The liberal tradition articulated by Olive Schreiner was to be reasserted in **Alan Paton**'s *Cry, The Beloved Country* (1948). More than any other piece of literature, this novel brought the tragedy of apartheid to the world's attention, and challenged South Africans to confront their prejudices. Paton, a leader of the nonracial Liberal Party, went on to write *Too Late the Phalarope* (1952), which dealt with interracial sex and personal tragedy in an Afrikaner community, and *Ah But Your Land is Beautiful* (1981), which is generally regarded as a good story but lacking the power of the two earlier novels.

The liberal sensibility continued in the work of **Nadine Gordimer** and **Dan Jacobson**, both of whom secured an international reputation in the 1950s. Jacobson's work – *The Trap* (1955), *A Dance in the Sun* (1956), *The Price of Diamonds* (1957) and *The Rape of Tamar* (1970) – reflected the troubled consciousness of a white South African, but it was Gordimer who was to establish her reputation as 'the conscience of white South Africa', and who was the only South African writer to come near Alan Paton in global stature. From the 1950s to the present time, Gordimer has used her writing to explore personal relationships within the context of a changing society. Gordimer's novels provide a magnificent historical and social record. They include *Lying Days* (1953), *A World of Strangers* (1958), *Occasion for Loving* (1963), *The Late Bourgeois World* (1966), *A Guest of Honour* (1971), *The Conservationist* (1974), *Burger's Daughter* (1979), *July's People* (1981), *A Sport of Nature* (1987), *My Son's Story* (1990), and *None to Accompany Me* (1994). In 1991 her international reputation was confirmed when she was awarded the Nobel Prize for Literature.

The other South African writer with a formidable international reputation is **JM Coetzee**, author of *Dusklands* (1974), *In the Heart of the Country* (1977), *The Life and Times of Michael K* (1983), *Waiting for the Barbarians* (1980), *Age of Iron* (1990), *Boyhood* (1997), *Disgrace* (1999), *Youth* (2002) and *Madame Costello* (2003). Like Gordimer, Coetzee was awarded the Nobel Prize for Literature (in 2003). Coetzee recently stirred controversy with his emigration to Australia, and with his depiction of life in post-apartheid South Africa in his novel *Disgrace*.

Other, many other, contemporary English-speaking writers have engaged with the complexities of South African life under apartheid and in the transition to democracy, and have a measure of international

THE WOW FACTOR!

South African novelist **JM Coetzee** *was the first person ever to win the Man Booker Prize twice – in 1983 for* The Life and Times of Michael K *and in 1999 for* Disgrace. *This achievement was matched only by his Nobel Prize for Literature in 2003.*

acclaim. They include the poet Douglas Livingstone; Damon Galgut (*Sinless Season, A Good Doctor*); Christopher Hope (*A Separate Development, White Boy Running* and *My Chocolate Redeemer*); Pamela Jooste (*Dance with a Poor Man's Daughter*); Jo-Ann Richard (*The Innocence of Roast Chicken*); Gillian Slovo (*Ties of Blood*); Rian Malan (*My Traitor's Heart*); Mark Behr (*The Smell of Apples* and *Embrace*); and Johnny Steinberg (*Midlands*).

Writers in ferment

There is also a rich body of English literature produced by black South Africans, although they have struggled against a grievous lack of resources.

The first significant novel by an indigenous author was *Mhudi*, written in 1920 by ANC founder **Sol Plaatje**, although published only in 1930. *Mhudi* was a tragic love story set on the highveld during the *mfecane*, a time of devastation and conflict in the early 19th century. Then came the Zulu playwright and poet **Herbert Dhlomo**, who combined Western literary modes with an African cosmology in works such as his long poem, 'The Valley of a Thousand Hills' (1941).

Rapid urbanisation in the 1930s and 1940s displaced millions of black Africans and created massive problems of personal and social identity. These issues are reflected in the novels of a 'coloured' South African **Peter Abrahams** (see *Mine Boy*, 1946, and *A Wreath for Udomo*,1956). Despite the confusion and technical deficiencies of his work, Abraham provided inspiration for the new wave of African writing that erupted from the cultural ferment of **Sophiatown**. The vehicle for the new urban literature was *Drum* magazine, which started in 1951: its journalists – Can Themba, Bloke Modisane, Nat Nakasa, Casey Motsisi, Arthur Maimane, Lewis Nkosi, and Todd Matshikiza – have passed into legend. Their vibrant, racy style of writing, and their frantic lives, were iconic of the 'jazz decade'. These talented, courageous individuals lived by the maxim, 'live fast, die young, and have a good-looking corpse', and, almost to the man, they died in tragic circumstances. They left a wealth of short stories and journalism, and a great musical – Matshikiza's *King Kong*.

The one surviving writer associated with Sophiatown is **Es'kia Mphahlele**, who produced *Down Second Avenue* (in 1959), an important semi-autobiographical novel set in the bustling slum of Marabastad in Pretoria. Mphahlele was to publish numerous short stories, poems, and critical essays in a long career that has included many years as professor of literature at Wits.

Other places connected with forced removal and the liberation struggle also inspired a compelling literature. **Ahmed Essop**, for example, produced several collections of humorous but poignant stories that captured the vibrant and colourful life of the Indian community of Fordsburg, prior to their exile to distant Lenasia. District Six in Cape Town provoked **Richard Rive** to write *Buckingham Palace* and *Emergency* (1964), and **Alex La Guma** to pen *A Walk in the Night* (1962).

The radicals

The next wave of African writing emerged with the rise of the Black Consciousness movement (BCM) in the 1970s, and was more obviously political than the writings of the 1950s. **Steve Biko**, prophet of the BCM, was to declare his manifesto in *I Write What I Like* (1978).

The Soweto uprising of 1976 provoked a radical poetry and a cluster of novels that were described by Don Mattera as 'angry, anguished and articulate'. They include Wally Serote's *To Every Birth its Blood* (1981), Sipho Sepamla's *A Ride in the Whirlwind* (1981), and Miriam Tlali's *Amandla* (1981). The literature of resistance continued into the 1980s, supported by defiant publications such as the journal *Staffrider*. Many authors of this genre were not formally schooled in the conventions of writing, and were criticised for their lack of technical proficiency, but they did succeed in creating a powerful new form of expression.

One important trend during the recent past has been the emergence of a number of female writers, among them Miriam Tlali, Ellen Kuzwayo, author of *Call Me Woman* (1985), and Bessie Head, whose brilliant and agonised works, notably *Where Rain Clouds Gather* (1969) and *A Question of Power* (1973), were written in exile in Serowe, Botswana.

On of the most controversial of modern black writers is the 'people's poet', **Mzwakhe Mbuli**, who swept to prominence in the 1980s with his performance verse at political gatherings and mass funerals. Mbuli was detained on a number of occasions, and survived several assassination attempts. An indication of his prestige was the role he played as praise singer in introducing President Mandela at his 1994 inauguration ceremony. However, in 1997 he was charged and convicted as an accomplice to armed robbery. Mbuli, who was recently released, has pleaded his innocence, insisting he was framed.

Today, there is a new generation of black (and Indian) writers who are engaging with a society in transition: Phaswane Mpe (*Welcome to Our Hillbrow*); Zakes Mda (*Heart of Redness* and *The Madonna of Excelsior*); K Sello Duiker (*The Quiet Violence of Dreams*); Ashraf Jamal (*Love Theme in the Wilderness*); Achmat Dangor (*Kafka's Curse* and *Bitter Fruit*); Imraan Coovadia (*The Wedding*); and Tatamkhulu Afrika (*Bitter Eden*). Sadly, both Phaswane Mpe and K Sello Duiker died recently.

Writers in Afrikaans

Much of the rich tradition of Afrikaans literature is not easily accessible to the international visitor, although many of the most important works have been translated into English. The extent and variety of the canon is remarkable given that Afrikaans was formally recognised as a language separate from Dutch only in the early 20th century.

The recurring theme in this body of literature is the ongoing tension between the individual writer and the identity of the *volk* (Afrikaner nation). **CJ Langenhoven** – author of *Die Stem van Suid-Afrika*, which became the national anthem after South Africa was declared a Republic in 1961 – played a key role in promoting a *volk* mythology through his emotive poetry, but other writers have had a more uneasy relationship with Afrikanerdom.

Eugene Marais, for example, reacted to the narrowness of Afrikaner Calvinism in his pseudo-scientific works, *The Soul of the White Ant* and *My Friend the Baboons*, which drew on both Darwinism and Bushman folklore, while the gay writer Louis Leipoldt, author of *Stormwrack*, was an active supporter of the suffragette movement. NP van Wyk Louw – who was to become professor of Afrikaans in Amsterdam, and who wrote *Raki* (1941) and *Germanicus* (1956) – espoused a 'liberal nationalism', concerned with the 'just survival' of the Afrikaner nation. DJ Opperman was also to struggle with his relationship to the *volk*; he was, for example, to be accused of blasphemy for presenting the baby Jesus as coloured in his poem 'Kersliedjie'. Etienne Leroux's irreverent *Magersfontein O Magersfontein* tells of promiscuous sex among the makers of a film on a historic Anglo-Boer War battle.

However, of the leading Afrikaans authors it was only Breyten Breytenbach and André Brink who directly denounced apartheid, and suffered the consequences. Brink's *Kennis Van Die Aand* (1974) was the first Afrikaans novel to be banned, while Breytenbach was charged under the Terrorism Act, and imprisoned for seven years.

Breytenbach's works, now translated into English, include *The True Confessions of an Albino Terrorist* (1984) and *Memory of Snow and Dust* (1989). Brink translated his own novels into English – *An Instant in the Wind* (1976), *Rumours of Rain* (1978), *A Dry White Season* (1979), *A Chain of Voices* (1982), *States of Emergency* (1988), *The First Life of Adamaster* (1993), *Devil's Valley* (1998), and *The Other Side of Silence* (2002). Other protesting voices have come from the Afrikaner poet Ingrid Jonker, who commited suicide by drowning at the age of 31, and the 'coloured' Afrikaner Adam Small. An important recent contribution to transitional South Africa was Antjie Krog's *Country of My Skull*, which recounts stories told to the Truth and Reconciliation Commission.

ARCHITECTURE

Premodern architecture in South Africa is rich and varied. It ranges from Zulu 'beehive' kraals and colourful Ndebele homesteads to the elegant simplicity of Cape Dutch homesteads and small-town Karoo cottages. The Western Cape is especially known for its early architecture, providing many examples of the Cape Dutch style that dates from the 17th century.

British rule at the Cape and in Natal introduced the colonial Victorian idiom, with all its frills and quaintness. An excellent example is the ornate City Hall in Pietermaritzburg, but there are many others. In the Boer republics of the Transvaal and the Free State the building style was stolid and stern and has been described as 'North European Wilhelminian' (see the buildings around Pretoria's Church Square and along Brand Street in Bloemfontein). Equally impressive are the grand Edwardian, Georgian and neo-Classical buildings of Johannesburg, built with mining capital.

The finest architecture of the late 19th and early 20th centuries was that of Sir Herbert Baker, who succeeded magnificently in blending British period styles with South African landscape and materials. His most important commission was the design of the Union Buildings in Pretoria, which remains one of South Africa's most elegant buildings.

In the 1930s **Art Deco** was a common style in Cape Town, Durban, and the Witwatersrand, and many of these buildings have survived. By the late 1930s, however, the **Modern** movement (or International style) of Le Corbusier and Mies van der Rohe was revolutionising architectural thinking in South Africa, largely as a result of the evangelising efforts of **Rex Martienssen** at the University of the Witwatersrand. Le Corbusier himself recognised the importance of Martienssen and his associates, and labelled them the 'Transvaal Group'. By the late 1940s, however, Transvaal architects such as Norman Hansen and Roy Kantorowich were refining and softening the severity of Martienssen's modernism.

Changing styles
New York was the model for the development of South Africa's inner cities, and especially for Johannesburg. However, there were other influences, such as Oscar Niemeyer's brand of Brazilian modernism, evident for example in Johannesburg's suburb of Hillbrow (which went high-rise in the 1950s).

As the Transvaal Group mellowed and found a more regional expression, so emerged a new and severe form of architecture associated with Afrikaner nationalism. Its first great symbol, the Voortrekker Monument outside Pretoria, was completed in the late 1940s. The buildings in this idiom were often massive and intimidating. Also associated with the period was the construction of the vast segregated townships of box-like houses built in endless repetition.

From the 1980s **post-Modern** architecture began to offset the severity of Modernism but, unhappily, instead of exploring the local context it served mainly as a vehicle for rampant consumer capitalism, and for increasingly strange developments that seem to have less and less connection with South Africa. One of the earliest and, perhaps still, the most extravagant of its representations is Sun City, north of Rustenburg in the old homeland of Bophuthatswana. After 1994, casino architecture moved from the rural homeland areas into the cities, reaching, perhaps, it most bizarre and inauthentic limit in the MonteCasino complex in Fourways, Johannesburg, a fake Italian hillside village.

In sharp contrast to the preposterous new architecture of casinos and shopping centres are the spaces and buildings of the shack settlements that are a common feature in South Africa's towns and cities. Gradually a new architecture is emerging that recognises the value of learning from ways in which people create their own living environments, often in very difficult circumstances.

READ ALL ABOUT IT!

• Clive Chipkins, Johannesburg Style (David Philip Publishers)
• Dennis Radford, A Guide to the Architecture of Durban and Pietermaritzburg (David Philip Publishers)
• SA Architect (monthly journal)
• Alan Lipman, Architecture On My Mind: Critical Readings in Design (Unisa Press)
• Hilton Judin and Ivan Vladislavic, BLANK: Architecture, Apartheid and After (Distributed Art Publishers)
• Christina Muwanga, Ellipsis Guide to Recent Architecture: South Africa (Ellipsis)
• Graham Viney and Alain Proust, Historic Houses of South Africa (Abbeville Press)

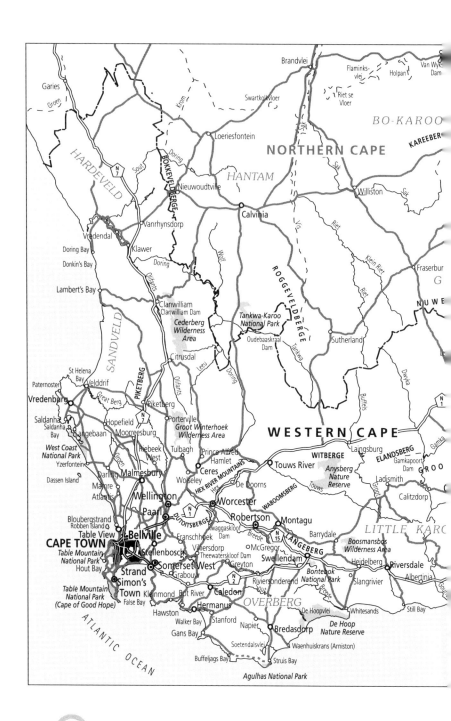

WESTERN CAPE

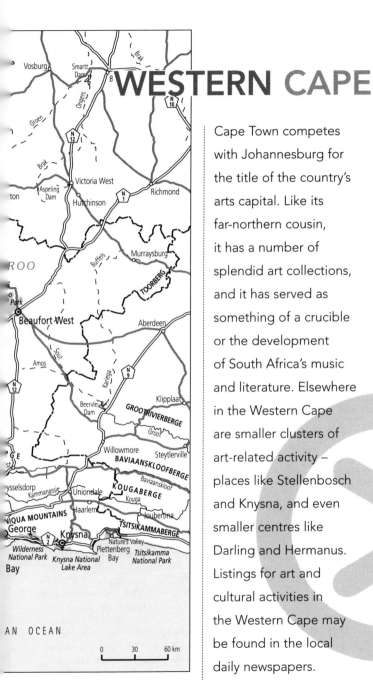

Cape Town competes with Johannesburg for the title of the country's arts capital. Like its far-northern cousin, it has a number of splendid art collections, and it has served as something of a crucible or the development of South Africa's music and literature. Elsewhere in the Western Cape are smaller clusters of art-related activity – places like Stellenbosch and Knysna, and even smaller centres like Darling and Hermanus. Listings for art and cultural activities in the Western Cape may be found in the local daily newspapers.

AFRICAN HERITAGE

The Western Cape is not known for visual displays of African indigenous culture, but the influx of migrants from the Xhosa heartland in the Eastern Cape has brought many traditional practices to the region. It is now not uncommon, for example, to see, within the cities, young initiates of the circumcision ritual covered in head to foot with chalk or clay. At the time of writing (2004) a multimillion-rand traditional village, **Freedom Park**, was being built near Khayelitsha, the vast township northeast of Cape Town. Plans to incorporate an initiation camp into the village (for circumcision ceremonies), however, provoked controversy.

Legend, the accommodation chain, recently established the **Khayalethu Cultural Village** near Plettenberg Bay. The enterprise offers insights into the traditional ways of the Xhosa people and incorporates a craft market, information centre, and a restaurant that serves both traditional and international food. Luxury accommodation is provided in the Whalesong Coastal Lodge.

THE VISUAL ARTS

Cape Town's more highly regarded pieces are held in Iziko Museums, a network of 15 showcase venues in and around the city. For the visual arts, the most important of these are the South African Museum (SAM), the South African National Gallery (SANG), the William Fehr Collection in the Castle of Good Hope and Rust en Vreugd, the Michaelis Collection, and the Natale Labia Museum.

The **South African Museum**, at 25 Queen Victoria Street, inaugurated in 1825, is the country's oldest and largest showcase. While the halls focus mainly on the natural sciences and anthropology, the place also houses some of the most beautiful examples of precolonial sculpture and painting in South Africa, including the mysterious Lydenburg Heads, the ancient Coldstream and Blombos stones, and the exquisitely beautiful Linton and Zamenkomst panels of rock art.

The **South African National Gallery** on Government Avenue, across the road from the Company's Garden, has a huge array of visual art – about 8 000 works altogether, most of them stored in vaults. The gallery rates as South Africa's premier art museum and has permanent collections of British, Dutch, French, Flemish, African, and South African works. The excellent collection of European art, which is of some importance internationally, is a product of the generosity of early patrons. In recent years the emphasis has shifted to African and South African art, both precolonial and contemporary, and the museum now has a valuable collection of indigenous sculpture and African beadwork. The most striking among the contemporary South African works is Jane Alexander's disturbing sculpture, *The Butcher Boys* (1985/86) – three menacing life-sized figures produced from mixed media (plaster, oil, bone and horn) that depict the horror and fear of life in South African townships during the state of emergency of the mid-1980.

MAKING CONTACT

Khayalethu Cultural Village (044) 533 5389; Whalesong Coastal Lodge (012) 346 2229, www.legendlodges.co.za; South African Museum (021) 481 3800, www.museums.org.za/sam; South African National Gallery (021) 467 4660, www.museums.org.za/sang

The **William Fehr Collection** is divided between the Castle of Good Hope and Rust en Vreugd. The collection, put together by Fehr, provides a fascinating window into life in the Dutch settlement at the Cape in the 17th and 18th centuries and during the British occupation up to the mid-19th century. It includes works by artists such as WHFL Langschmidt, Thomas Baines, and Thomas Bowler. **The Castle of Good Hope** on Buitenkant Street, completed in 1676 as the headquarters of the Dutch East India Company in the Cape, houses the collection in the rooms that lead off the Kat Balcony in the first courtyard. **Rust en Vreugd** at 78 Buitenkant Street, home to the rest of the collection, is a three-storey house built in the 1770s for the attorney-general of the Cape, William Cornelis Boers, although it was subsequently used as a school and teachers' training college. Today it is regarded as the best surviving example of an 18th-century Cape Dutch townhouse. It is graced by furnishings typical of the period, as well as by paintings, glass and silverware.

The **Michaelis Collection** in Old Town House, Greenmarket Square, houses a treasure-trove of 16th- to 18th-century artworks by Dutch and Flemish masters, among them Frans Hals, Jan Steen, Jacob Ruisdal, and Anthony van Dyck. The Old Town House (the early 'city hall') was built in 1755 in light and decorative rococo style and was one of the first double-storey structures in Cape Town. In 1905, however, it lost its status as the city hall to a new building on the Grand Parade, and, in 1913, was dedicated to housing an art collection donated by Max Michaelis that had originally been put together by Sir Hugh Lane, who was to become the director of the National Gallery of Ireland. The emphasis on Dutch and Flemish paintings is in recognition of the Dutch origins of the Cape settlement.

The **Natale Labia Museum**, on the Muizenberg Main Road in the southern Peninsula, was presented to the South African National Gallery by Count Natale Labia in memory of his parents, an Italian prince and princess. The design and furnishings of the house, built in 1930 to serve the Italian legation in South Africa, reflects the styles of 18th-century Venice. It now functions as an art museum, and a venue for temporary exhibitions, as well as a cultural centre that offers lectures, concerts, poetry readings, pottery workshops, and drawing classes.

The city's other important art showplace, the **Irma Stern Museum** in The Firs, Cecil Road, Rosebank, is managed by the University of Cape Town and features the work of South Africa's most respected woman artist. Irma Stern established her reputation in the 1930s and played an important role in reshaping South African art by challenging the traditional realism of the early colonial period. The museum, which was opened in 1971, is located in the house she occupied from 1927 until her death in 1966.

READ ALL ABOUT IT!

NEWSPAPERS
Listings for art and cultural activities in the Western Cape may be found in the Friday editions of following:
- *The Argus*
- *The Cape Times*
- *Mail & Guardian (weekly)*

WEBSITES
- *www.capetowntoday.co.za*
- *www.capetownevents.co.za*
- *www.chico.mweb.za/mg/*
- *www.tonight.co.za*

BOOKINGS
Computicket 083 915 8000, www.computicket.com

MAKING CONTACT

Castle of Good Hope
(021) 464 1261;
William Fehr Collection
(Rust en Vreugd)
(021) 465 3628, www. museums.org.za/wfc;
Michaelis Collection
(Old Town House)
(021) 481 3933, www. museums.org.za/michaelis;
Natale Labia Museum
(021) 788 4106/7, www. museums.org.za/natale;
Irma Stern Museum
(021) 685 5686

western cape

MAKING CONTACT

Greatmore Studios
(021) 447 9699,
www.greatmoreart.org;
Association for Visual
Arts (AVA) Metropolitan
Gallery (021) 424 7436,
www.ava.co.za;
Pan African Market
(021) 426 4478, www.
panafricanmarket.co.za;
Gugu S'Thebe
(021) 695 3493;
Sivuyile Tourism Centre
(021) 637 8449;
Philani Printing and
Weaving (021) 387 5124;
African Craft Market
(021) 361 5246;
Softserve at the South
African Art Gallery
(021) 465 5022,
www.public-eye.co.za;
PJ Olivier Art Centre
(021) 886 4854;
Sasol Art Museum
(021) 808 3693;
University of Stellenbosch
Art Gallery (021) 808 3524;
Spier Wine Estate
(021) 809 1100,
www.spier.co.za

Gallery spaces

City venues that provide studios and exhibition space for artists, and that are open to the public, include **Greatmore Studios** (47–49 Greatmore Street, Woodstock), Cape Town's equivalent of Johannesburg's Bag Factory, where local and international, emerging and established artists mix, provide mutual support and run outreach programmes.

There's also the Association for Visual Arts (AVA) **Metropolitan Gallery** at 35 Church Street, which has a large space for exhibiting the work of both emergent and established artists, for workshops, concerts and lectures, and which also runs an energetic outreach programme. For contemporary African arts and crafts visit the **Pan African Market** at 76 Long Street, described by *City Style* magazine as a 'rainbow labyrinth filled with exciting Africanalia'.

Much of the art is up-market and displayed in exclusive galleries. There are, however, spaces for arts and crafts in the townships, notably Gugu S'Thebe in **Langa**; Sivuyile Tourism Centre in **Gugulethu**; Philani Printing and Weaving in **Khayelitsha**; and the African Craft Market, also in Khayelitsha. Like Johannesburg, Cape Town has a public art project, **Public Eye**, which promotes the arts in the wider arena, in places visited by people who would normally not be seen at an art gallery. Public art projects have included the Spier outdoor sculpture biennial, the Robben Island human rights project, and Softserve at the South African Art Gallery, where young artists lay on temporary exhibitions as well as performances.

The country areas

The most important centre of the arts outside Cape Town and the Peninsula is the historic university town of **Stellenbosch**, home (among other things) to the Rembrandt van Rijn Foundation established in 1964 to promote an appreciation of South African art, and to introduce South Africans to the work of major international talent. It also has the PJ Olivier Art Centre, which occupies the 18th-century Rhenish Girls' School building and a number of museums and galleries clustered in and around the university, including the Sasol Art Museum, and the University of Stellenbosch Art Gallery.

The **Spier** estate at Lynedoch, outside Stellenbosch, has emerged as a cultural hub embracing many forms of art and is host to, for example, the Spier outdoor sculpture biennial convened by Cape Town-based Public Eye.

The Garden Route town of **Knysna** has attracted a significant number of studios and galleries. Artists have also clustered in and around **Hermanus** and other centres along the so-called 'Whale Route', and in the Boland mountains around **Franschhoek** and **McGregor**.

STAGE AND SCREEN

The official home of theatre in the Western Cape is the **Artscape** complex off DF Malan Street on Cape Town's Foreshore. It was opened as the Nico Malan theatre in 1971and comprises a huge, modern building – popularly known as 'the Nico' – which for long served as headquarters of the Cape Performing Arts Board

(CAPAB). Since 1999, however, the complex has been managed by a not-for-profit company. The once-staid, state-funded institution has been given a facelift, its main venues ranging from the cabaret-type space called Artscape on the Side, which seats about 100, to the 1 200-seater Opera House.

The second largest theatre space is the University of Cape Town's **Baxter** complex on Main Road, Rondebosch, established in 1977 from a bequest in support of the arts. Although a formal venue, it has provided great opportunities for young talent. Large productions are staged in the main auditorium (666 seats) and concert hall (638); the cozier Sanlam studio theatre (166) provides a venue for more experimental drama. The university also has a number of small alternative venues, among them the Arena and Little theatres.

Thirdly, there's Pieter Toerien's **Theatre on the Bay** in Camps Bay. Like the first two, this is a mainstream venue with a wide appeal, although it's not very large (220 seats). It does, however, have an alternative slant – the Cabaret Café, attached to the theatre, puts on more intimate productions and stages the work of newer, younger playwrights. For musicals, try the **Roxy Revue Bar** at GrandWest Casino in the so-called Northern Suburbs.

Alternative theatre

Although Cape Town has large and usually well-filled mainstream venues it also makes room for alternative and specialised theatre. Spaces include The **Independent Armchair Theatre** on Main Road, Observatory, home to the Cape Comedy Collective, a group of more than 30 comics; the **Labia** at 68 Orange Street, Gardens; **On Broadway**, at 21 Somerset Road, Green Point, which is in the heart of the 'gay village' and known for musical extravaganzas and drag shows; **The Warehouse**, at 6 Dixon Road, Green Point, known for its popular *Meet Joe Barber* and for experimental shows, among them *Shopping and Fucking* and *Naked Boys Singing*; **Off Moroka Café Africaine** in Adderley Street, with its off-the-wall productions; the funky **Obz Café** in Lower Main Road, Observatory; and, the rather run-down **Cape Town Theatre Laboratory**.

The townships of the **Cape Flats** are sadly lacking in facilities, but there is an informal township theatre. Perhaps the only relatively formal venue is the **Joseph Stone Theatre**, on Klipfontein Road.

The country areas

The major arts centre outside Cape Town is **Stellenbosch**. Oude Libertas, off Adam Tas Road, is an open-air theatre; the Dorp Street Theatre Café puts on shows as well as music and poetry readings. Very popular is the auditorium on the Spier estate.

The **Barnyard Theatre** was opened by Louis Moller and Sybel Coetzee in a converted barn on their farm near Plettenberg Bay. The informality proved popular and soon there were nine Barnyard theatres countrywide. In the Cape you'll find Barnyards on Aaskop farm near Plettenberg Bay, Rietvlei near Mossel Bay, and in Bridge House school, Franschhoek.

Perhaps the most unusual Cape venue is **Evita se Perron**, on the old railway platform in Darling (*see pages 32–33*).

MAKING CONTACT

Artscape
(dial-a-seat) (021) 421 7695,
(box office) (021) 421 7839,
www.artscape.co.za;
Baxter Theatre Complex
(021) 685 7880,
www.baxter.co.za;
Arena *and* **Little** *theatres*
(021) 480 7129;
Theatre on the Bay
(021) 438 3300/1, www.
theatreonthebay.co.za;
GrandWest Casino
(021) 505 7777;
Cape Comedy Collective
(021) 447 1514,
www.comedyclub.co.za;
The Labia
(021) 424 5927;
On Broadway
(021) 418 8338,
www.onbroadway.co.za;
The Warehouse
(021) 421 0777;
Off Moroka
Café Africaine
www.offmoroka.co.za;
Obz Café *(021) 448 5555;*
Cape Town Theatre
Laboratory *(021) 447 0854;*
Joseph Stone Theatre
(021) 637 1268;
Oude Libertas
(021) 809 7474,
www.oudelibertas.co.za;
Barnyard Theatre
(Plettenberg Bay)
082 973 1246,
(Rietvlei) (044) 698 1022,
(Bridge House)
(021) 874 1505), www.
barnyardtheatre.co.za

Alternative film

Cape Town is the film capital of South Africa, an increasingly popular location for international productions. The city also has numerous venues for watching mainstream and alternative film and video, and it hosts a number of screen festivals that are aimed by and large at those especially interested in 'art' or foreign-language cinema

Among the city's alternative venues are the Cinema Nouveau theatres in Cavendish Square in the suburb of Claremont, Cape Town and at the V&A Waterfront; the Independent Armchair Theatre at 135 Lower Main Road, Observatory; The Labia on Orange at 68 Orange Street, Gardens, and Labia on Kloof at the Lifestyles Centre on Park Road. For giant-screen movies see the IMAX theatre at the V&A Waterfront.

There's also the Pan African Video Centre on the first floor of the Pan African Market at 76 Long Street, where African videos can be watched or bought.

Film festivals include the Cape Town International, hosted by the University of Cape Town in November each year (to book, contact the festival organiser via e-mail or call Computicket); the Gay and Lesbian (see the companion volume *South Africa's Top Sites – Gay & Lesbian*), and the Molweni in the Cape Flats area, dedicated to developing the emerging township film industry (book through Computicket).

MAKING CONTACT

Cinema Nouveau
082 16789;
Independent Armchair
Theatre *(021) 447 1514;*
The Labia
(021) 424 5927,
www.labia.co.za;
IMAX *(Computicket)*
083 915 8000,
www.imax.co.za;
Cape Town
International
Film Festival
*filmfest@
hidden.uct.ac.za;*
Gay and Lesbian
Film Festival
(Computicket)
083 915 8000,
www.pmcnet.co.za/mol

Evita at Darling

A 45-minute drive from Cape Town is Darling, the small inland town most famous for its wild flowers, which carpet the countryside in springtime and draw tourists from afar afield. The other reason to visit this pretty little place, however, is Evita se Perron, the town's flamboyant cabaret venue, restaurant, bar and museum that reflects the positive, the tragic, and the absurd in South African life and history.

In 1997, satirist and cabaret artist Pieter-Dirk Uys (whose alter ego and drag character, Evita Bezuidenhout, has been described as 'the most famous white woman in South Africa') purchased the old station building in Darling and set about transforming it into a cultural hub and shrine to 'boere kitsch'.

Centrepiece of Evita se Perron is the theatre where Uys continues to stage his provocative shows. Among these have been *Dekaffirnated, Live from Boerassic Park, You ANC Nothing Yet, Tannie Evita Praat Kaktus,* and *Ouma Ossewania Praat Vuil* (all takes on clichéd Afrikaner iodiosyncracies and how these have evolved – or not – in the 'new' South Africa). The satire is acute and confrontational. In the past, Uys provided an intensely political commentary but today, however, he also tackles the sexual. His show *Foreign Aids*, for example, is a powerful, painful and hilarious engagement with the tragedy of HIV/Aids, a show that developed out of a series of Aids workshops that he conducted with children across the country.

THE SOUNDS OF MUSIC

Cape Town is home to such jazz greats as Abdullah Ibrahim and Chris McGregor. With so many jazz festivals, the city is known as the 'New Orleans of Africa'.

The history of jazz in the Western Cape is closely tied to the story of **District Six**, the inner suburb so brutally demolished by the apartheid regime during the 1960s and 1970s. Described as 'a place where music reigned', District Six was an extraordinary melting pot that produced a unique blend of sounds – the *ghoemma* of the coloured community fused with American jazz, Latin dance and African styles, such as jive, *marabi* and *mbaqanga*, to produce the Cape jazz that we know today (see page 34).

Premier occasions

The year's biggest musical event is the **Cape Town International Jazz Festival** (previously North Sea Jazz Festival), sponsored by Standard Bank Joy of Jazz and held in March at the International Convention Centre. This is the southern hemisphere's version of its namesake, held annually in The Hague. Although initiated only in 1999, the local celebration already attracts 25 000 devotees, and it's regarded as an important part of the international jazz circuit. Other events include Jazzathon at the V&A Waterfront (January), Jazzathon on Robben Island (February), and Jol met Jazz in Oudtshoorn (April). Summer concerts at Kirstenbosch botanical gardens also commonly feature jazz.

MAKING CONTACT

Cape Town International Jazz Festival *(the North Sea Jazz Festival)* *(Computicket)* *083 915 8000, www.nsjfcapetown.com;* **Joy of Jazz** *www.joyofjazz.co.za;* **Jazzathon** and **Jol met Jazz** *www.jazzathon.co.za;* **Kirstenbosch** *(021) 799 8783/8620, www.nbi.co.za*

Pieter-Dirk Uys remains South Africa's most compelling satirist. As a recent visitor to Darling observed, 'his theatre of laughter is one of the most dangerous places in the world, for when you laugh your defences are down. You are sitting in the dark, feeling safe and secret, and then you see or hear something that makes you laugh. And in that moment your laughter gives your innermost self away. Your attitudes and beliefs are suddenly exposed and you feel naked and somehow healed' (Stacey Sachs).

Evita se Perron bustles with activity. While waiting for a show you can browse in the Bapetikosweti duty-free shop, sip beer in Bambi's Berlin Bar, and enjoy traditional South African fare – tomato *bredie*, chicken curry, waterblommetjies, bobotie, koeksisters – in Evita se Kombuis restaurant.

It feels as if the whole of South Africa's apartheid past is written into the walls of Evita se Perron. It does so in a way that makes you laugh, and understand the ridiculousness of it all. The garden, called the HF Verwoerd Marine Reserve (also known as Boerassic Park) is home to gnomes and satirical sculptures, one of apartheid cabinet minister Piet Koornhof, whom Pieter-Dirk loved to lampoon, and another of an oxwagon being pulled by a jet and a satellite in the shape of *potjie* (a traditional Afrikaner cooking pot). In one of the toilets there's a shrine to ultra-rightwinger Eugene Terreblanche – you look up at the giant portrait as you sit on the loo and suddenly it all makes sense!

AND WHAT'S MORE...

An evening at **Evita se Perron** *is local entertainment at its finest, and well worth the trip to the small inland town of Darling. For bookings and enquiries, contact the theatre on (022) 492 2831/51, bookings@evita.co.za, www.evita.co.za; or call the* **Darling Tourist Information Office** *on (022) 492 3361.*

western cape

MAKING CONTACT

'169 on Long'
(021) 426 1107;
Kennedy's Cigar Bar
(021) 424 1212;
Mama Africa
(021) 424 8634;
Green Dolphin
(021) 421 7471;
GrandWest Casino
(021) 505 7465;
Cape Town Tourism
(021) 426 4260,
www.cape-town.org;
Thuthuka Tours
(021) 637 4232;
Cape Town Festival
(021) 465 1166, www.
capetownfestival.co.za;
Klein Karoo
Nasionale Kunstefees
(044) 203 8600,
www.kknk.co.za;
Urban Voices
International Arts Festival
(011) 726 6916,
www.artsexchange.co.za;
Spier *(021) 809 1165,*
www.spier.co.za

The CBD and V&A Waterfront host many clubs and restaurants featuring live jazz performances. Along **Long Street** alone are '169 on Long', Kennedy's Cigar Bar and Mama Africa, with its marimba bands. At the **V&A Waterfront** is the Green Dolphin restaurant that features nightly jazz while the GrandWest Casino has regular jazz in the Hanover Street venue.

Visitors may also experience jazz in the townships. *A Jazz Route Guide* is available from the Cape Town tourism offices and there are also **musical tours** as, for example, that conducted by Muse Art Journeys, developed by the City of Cape Town and the New World Music Foundation, and the Evening Jazz Tour conducted by Thuthuka Tours.

EVENTS

The **Cape Town Festival** aims to place the city alongside Rio de Janeiro and Sydney as one of southern hemisphere's festive capitals. It's held in March and is full of music, visual art, theatre, dance, film, literature, drama and comedy. It was inaugurated in 1999 as an exuberant attempt to bring together the diversity of urban cultures in a common celebration around the 'One City, Many Cultures' theme. The centre of festivities is in the 350-year old Company's Garden, but there are activities throughout the city, suburbs and townships. Included within its broad ambit is the Cape Town Month of Photography, the Trade Winds Literary Festival and the Children's Film Festival.

The music of District Six

In District Six a polyglot of cultures intermingled, inspiring new forms of art. In its early years freed slaves, their forefathers brought from Java, India, Malaya, Madagascar, West Africa and Mozambique, mixed with the indigenous Khoekhoen, and with Dutch and English settlers.

David Coplan, in his book *In Township Tonight!*, describes how the Khoekhoen used the drum, the *khais*, together with the seaweed trumpet, an imitation of the European bugle made from kelp, to produce melodies of their new folk songs, and also how the *rankie*, a three- or four-stringed plucked guitar, was introduced by the Malabar slaves.

Before segregation was entrenched, there was a crossover between the folk songs of the Dutch and the *ghoemmaliedjies* of the Malay, and when the English took control in 1806 they brought styles such as the English country dance, the 'rainbow ball' and the military marching band.

By the late 19th century, itinerant Cape coloured musicians travelled the interior, and especially to Kimberley, where they came into contact with traditional African music of the mineworkers, and also with the honky-tonky piano style of the American prospectors.

But the biggest influence on the music of the Western Cape were the spirituals and stage performances of black American minstrels. In 1887, 'McAdoo's American Jubilee Singers' visited the Cape and made an enormous impression on the local population. They were to return at least three times, and inspired widespread local imitation.

The other major occasion is the **Klein Karoo Nasionale Kunstefees** (KKNK), which takes place in May in the Little Karoo town of Oudtshoorn. It represents the Afrikaans alternative to the National Festival of Arts in Grahamstown. Legend has it that the KKNK was a product of an outburst by Oudtshoorn millionaire Nic Barrow, who was unable to find a table at a restaurant during the Grahamstown event. It currently includes about 200 productions featuring 1 000 artists, with ticket sales of more than 160 000, up from the 30 000 in 1995 when it was first held. It's now one of the largest events on the South African arts calendar but it has had mixed reviews. It tends to be rather boozy and rowdy, and still quite conservative, with far less cultural diversity than Grahamstown or, indeed, than the other major Afrikaans festival, the Aardklop Nasionale Kunstefees, which is held in the northern city of Potchefstroom.

Other festivals are more specialist or local than these two. The highly popular jazz occasions have already been discussed (see pages 33–34). **The Urban Voices International Arts Festival**, jointly hosted by Johannesburg and Cape Town in July and August, brings together black artists from Africa and the diaspora in celebration of African art and culture and features jazz, reggae, slam dance, theatre, the spoken word, and rumba. Increasingly popular is the **Spier Summer Festival** on the beautiful Spier wine estate near Stellenbosch, which offers five months of music, opera, dance, stand-up comedy and theatre.

Around the country

The **Hermanus Whale Festival** takes place in September/October, when the great southern rights calve offshore, and features a variety of arts (and a children's festival), plus music ranging from jazz and the classics to 'boere rock'. It has been billed as the ultimate in the 'enviro-art' experience.

Darling is host to the **Hello Darling Arts Festival**, which coincides with the wild flower show in September each year.

Knysna is host to at least three festivals each year. The Pink Loerie Festival usually takes place in May and is a flashy arts and culture carnival targeted at the gay and lesbian community. There's also the Nederburg Knysna Arts Experience in September, and, in the first part of July, the Kynsna Oyster Festival, a 10-day outdoor experience (sponsored by the Navy) noted for its oyster-eating and cooking competitions and for cabaret, comedy and sports.

The West Coast community of Atlantis hosts a celebration of music and comedy in November; the Up the Creek Music Festival takes place on a farm along the Breede River near Swellendam, and follows the pattern set by KwaZulu-Natal's Splashy Fen Music Festival.

At the annual Cape Gourmet Festival, celebrity chefs from across the world come together with a number of local chefs to produce a 'smorgasbord of talent and taste experience'. The type of celebration is mirrored in a number of similarly themed food festivals in and around the Cape throughout the year. For some idea of the sort of festivals on offer, see top right.

THE WOW FACTOR!

- *Caledon: Bread and Beer Festival (March)*
- *Uniondale: Apple Festival (March)*
- *Hermanus: Perlemoen Festival (March)*
- *Prince Albert: Olive Festival (April)*
- *Paarl: Nouveau Wine Festival (April)*
- *Malmesbury: Swartland Festival (June)*
- *Calitzdorp: Port Festival (July)*
- *Cape Town: Wine Festival (August)*
- *Citrusdal: Citrus Festival (September)*
- *Robertson Valley: Food Festival (October)*
- *Stellenbosch Food and Wine Festival (October)*
- *Somerset West: Strawberry Festival (December)*

MAKING CONTACT

Hermanus Whale Festival *(028) 313 0928, www.whalefestival.co.za;* **Hello Darling Arts Festival** *(022) 492 2831, www.evita.co.za;* **Pink Loerie Festival** *(044) 382 7768, www.gatmay.co.za;* **Nederburg Knysna Arts Experience** *www.artsinknysna.co.za;* **Kynsna Oyster Festival** *(044) 382 5510,* **Atlantis Festival** *(021) 572 1872;* **Up the Creek** *www. upthecreek.mweb.co.za*

Carnival time

By the late19th century the music of the saloons and gambling halls of Cape Town, and especially of District Six, was a jovial blend of Khoekhoen, African, Malay, Dutch, English and American popular music. Many coloured men followed the example of American minstrels in setting up their own performance clubs, with names such as the Meadow Cottonfield Jazz Singers and the Fabulous Orange Plantation Minstrels. Each New Year these different bands would dress up in their distinctive outfits and take to the streets singing their *ghoemmaliedjies* to the merry accompaniment of whistles, banjos, guitars, drums and tambourines. This was the great Cape Coon Carnival that continues to this day (it's now called the Cape Minstrel Festival, and takes place on 1, 2, 6 and 13 January each year) although the destruction of District Six took much of the heart and soul out of the merriment.

The popular music of the Western Cape was carried by coloured minstrels to other parts of the country, including Johannesburg where it was to have an influence on the development of township jazz and of popular music more generally. The Coon Carnival, for example, spread to Malay Camp in Kimberley and to Vrededorp in Johannesburg, and by the early 20th century the focus of musical innovation had shifted from District Six to the Witwatersrand.

But the traditions of District Six continued to influence music throughout South Africa. The most respected jazz musician South Africa has produced, **Abdullah Ibrahim** (initially known as Dollar Brand), was born in the District and was deeply affected and influenced by his life there, as one can clearly hear in the haunting, nostalgia-filled music of his song *District Six* in his famous album *African Magic*.

The community of District Six was to be destroyed by the apartheid removals of the 1970s, and a place Ibrahim described as a 'blazing swamp fire of satire sound' became 'empty, forlorn, and cobwebbed with gloom'.

THE PRINTED WORD

The Western Cape has a very impressive literary tradition. The more illuminating of the early works include the fairly recently (1973) compiled and published *The Letters of Lady Anne Barnard to Henry Dundas from the Cape and Elsewhere*, 1793–1803, and the *The Cape Journals of Lady Anne Barnard* (1995). Lady Anne was wife to the colonial secretary to the Colony at the end of the 18th century, and her writings now provide us with some insight into the mood and life of her era. At around the same time, **Thomas Pringle** captured social tensions and drama of the Cape landscape:
'O Cape of Storms!
although thy front be dark
And bleak thy naked cliffs and
   cheerless vales
And perilous thy fierce and
   faithless gales…
Yet, spite of physical and moral ill
And after all I've seen and suffered
   here
There are strong links that bind
me to thee still' (abstract courtesy
Michael Chapman, *A Century of South African Poetry*, AD Donker).

Local settings

In 20th-century literature Cape Town featured as a setting for the novels of Nobel Prize winner **JM Coetzee**, professor at the University of Cape Town before moving to Australia. One of his themes is the long journey; and, usually, it's a journey from Cape Town. *Dusklands* (1974) takes the reader north to the 'Land of the Great Namaqua', while in the *Life and Times of Michael K* (1983) the tragic Michael takes his ailing mother on the long road from Cape Town to Prince Albert during a civil war. Coetzee's more recent novel, *Disgrace* (1999), begins in a Cape Town university where a 52-year-old professor has an affair with a young student, and moves to a farm near Salem in the Eastern Cape. The city also features in the work of another local professor, **André Brink**, whose *Rights of Desire* explores Cape Town's seedy side in a tale of jaded love affairs, incest, murder, rape and persecution.

The decades of Struggle and oppression in Cape Town has inspired some fine literature. **Athol Fugard**'s play *The Island* (1973) is based on the grim role played by Robben Island; **Elsa Joubert**'s *The Long Journey of Poppie Nongena* (1978) is set in the townships of the Western, Eastern, and Northern Cape.

It is District Six, however, that seems to have had the greatest impact on South African literature. Two notable writers were **Alex La Guma** and **Richard Rive**. La Guma's short novel *A Walk in the Night* (1962) explored both the wretchedness and vibrancy of the area, but his most brilliant portrayal of life was probably *And a Threefold Cord* (1964). La Guma was a leading member of the South African Communist Party and treason trialist who died, in 1985, in exile in Havana, Cuba. He had lived in District Six as a child.

Richard Rive also spent childhood days in the District, and the area featured in his early novel *Emergency* (1964) and in his collection of short stories *Advance Retreat* (1983). It is most prominent, however, in his book *Buckingham Palace* (1986), a sensitive account of the complexities and contradictions of life before the removals. It was written 'so that we do not forget'. Tragically, however, Rive was murdered in his home at Princess Vlei, Cape Town, in 1989, at the age of 59.

District Six has also been the subject of many other works, both fictional and non-fictional, and has also inspired at least two excellent musicals – Taliep Petersen and David Kramer's *District Six* (1986), and their follow-up, *Kat and the Kings* (1999), which had a highly successful season in London, winning the Laurence Olivier Award for the best new musical of the year.

Today, District Six is still largely open space, but new developments are gradually reducing the emptiness. A powerful representation of the past is the **District Six Museum**, which occupies the old Central Methodist mission church at 24a Buitenkant Street. The museum provides an excellent introduction to the art, music and literature of this great icon of the South African struggle story.

AND WHAT'S MORE...

John Kannemeyer of Stellenbosch University and Wium van Zyl of the University of the Western Cape conduct Afrikaans literary tours in the Western and Northern Cape, which they call **Storietoere** *('story tours'). For bookings, contact them on (021) 976 5755.*

AND WHAT'S MORE...

While the streets and buildings of old District Six are long gone, and the lively banter of its residents no longer echo around the City Bowl, the spirit of the place lingers on in what is now the **District Six Museum**. *This fascinating archive of life in the area is housed at 24A Buitenkant Street (in the Central Methodist Mission Church). Contact the museum on (021) 461 8745, www.districtsix.co.za*

Rural life

The country areas have also made their contribution. Author **Pauline Smith** captured the essence of life in the remote rural Afrikaner settlements of the Little Karoo in *The Beadle* (1926) and *Platkops Children* (1935); the late **Dalene Matthee**, who was born in Riversdale in 1938, set her stories in the forests around Knysna. Matthee wrote of the destruction of the forest's elephant herds, and of the people of the area in *Circles in the Forest* and *Fiela's Child*. The Clanwilliam and Cederberg areas are the setting for the work of Afrikaans author **C Louis Leipoldt**, whose work is well exemplified in his *Stormwrack*, published post-humously in English in 1980.

Breyten Breytenbach – once a political prisoner and author of *The True Confessions of an Albino Terrorist* (1984) and *Memory of Snow and Dust* (1989) – was born in Bonnievale and educated in Wellington. His *Dog Heart* is a 'travel memoir' that draws on the memories of his youth in the Cape.

Also associated with the Western Cape is the Afrikaans writer **NP van Wyk Louw**, who lectured at the University of Cape Town and established a chair in Afrikaans in Amsterdam; and poet and playwright **Uys Krige**, who grew up near Swellendam and studied at Stellenbosch University.

Herman Charles Bosman was born in Kuils River, close to Cape Town, but his stories are set in Johannesburg and in the Groot Marico of North West province.

A remarkable setting for a contemporary novel is **Gamkaskloof** ('Die Hel'), which inspired André Brink's *Devil's Valley* (see page 40).

ARCHITECTURE

Cape Dutch homesteads, with their curved gables, thatched roofs and white-washed walls, are among the world's most graceful buildings. Perhaps the best known is **Groot Constantia**, the elegant manor house that belonged to Cape governor Simon van der Stel. It was built in 1685 and is a showcase offering a fascinating insight into 17th- and 18th-century settler life. The beautiful pediment gable of the adjoining cellar (which serves as a wine museum) is by sculptor Anton Anreith. Smaller but also elegant and open to the public are **Klein Constantia** and **Buitenverwachting**, which houses one of the country's top restaurants.

Outside Cape Town are many other lovely Cape Dutch home-steads, many of them venues along the various wine routes. Among the most attractive is **Vergelegen** in Somerset West, built by controversial Dutch East India Company governor Willem Adriaan van der Stel in 1699 and restored by Lady Florence Phillips in 1917. The camphor trees that Van der Stel planted still provide shade to visitors.

The **Spier** estate between Somerset West and Stellenbosch, which has already been mentioned for its contribution to art and culture (see page 35), is another lovely cluster of Cape Dutch farm buildings, including a handsome restored homestead that now serves as an art museum.

Stellenbosch is surrounded by historic wine estates, notable among which are Rustenburg, with its gabled milking shed, Neethlingshof, Blaauwklippen, Overgaauw, Morgenhof, Simonsig and Lievland.

Wineland gems

Founded in 1679 by the Dutch East India Company's Simon van der Stel, Stellenbosch is the country's second oldest colonial settlement (after Cape Town). The largest concentration of historic edifices is around De Braak, the village square in the middle of town, but many other beautiful buildings are to be found along the oak-lined streets that lead out from the centre. Particularly charming are those along Dorp Street.

The venerable town of **Paarl**, to the north of Stellenbosch, has also been well endowed by the past, especially along its lengthy Main Street (the Paarl Museum building is notable for its gable, which dates back to 1787). About 30 km from Paarl and Stellenbosch is the extraordinarily beautiful little town of **Franschhoek**, founded, in a fertile valley surrounded by rugged mountains, by the French Huguenots who had fled persecution in their home country in the late 17th century. Cape Dutch architecture meets French style and cuisine on the surrounding farms and estates, notable among which are Cabrière, Mont Rochelle, Chamonix, Grand Provence, La Motte and Boschendal.

The streets of **Tulbagh**, the town over the Bain's Kloof Pass, are lined with simple 17th- and 18th-century Cape Dutch cottages. In 1969 a devastating earthquake destroyed many of the buildings, but these have since been lovingly reconstructed. The other town with a fine Cape Dutch heritage is **Swellendam**, established just after Stellenbosch. The buildings, some dating back to 1745, are clustered around the Drostdy Museum in Swellengrebel Street.

The homesteads on the wine estates and the edifices in towns such as Stellenbosch and Swellendam represent the wealth and power of the Dutch East India Company elite. However, there are also buildings from this period – homes to poor, mainly mixed-race communities – that are enchanting in their simplicity. Some of the most charming spots are the **fishing villages** of Arniston (Waenhuiskrans) and Hotagterklip near Cape Agulhas, with their historic whitewashed cottages. Also lovely are the 18th- and 19th-century **mission stations**, notably Genadendal (1738), Mamre (1808), Wuppertal (1830), and Elim (1834) (see also the companion volume *South Africa's Top Sites – Spiritual*)

The city scene

The biggest collection of historic buildings is to be seen in Cape Town itself, many dating back to the period before the great and hugely destructive fires of 1736 and 1798. The **Castle of Good Hope**, off Buitenkant Street, was completed in 1676 in the style favoured for fortifications in Europe of the time. The interior was eventually decorated in the British Regency idiom. The Castle, which is open to the public, contains valuable collections of military history, furnishings and artworks, including part of the noted William Fehr Collection. Close by is the **Grand Parade**, once a military parade ground but now a bustling market space, perhaps best known as the place where Nelson Mandela gave his first speech following his release from prison in 1990. Dominating the square is Cape Town's Edwardian City Hall (1905).

MAKING CONTACT

Cabrière
(021) 876 2630;
Mont Rochelle
(021) 876 3000;
Chamonix
(021) 876 2498;
Grand Provence
(021) 876 3195;
La Motte
(021) 876 3119;
Boschendal
(021) 870 4270;
Tulbagh Tourism Office
(023) 230 1348,
www.tulbagh.com;
Drostdy Museum
(Swellendam Tourism)
(028) 514 2770;
Castle of Good Hope
(William Fehr Collection)
(021) 787 1249

The secret valley

André Brink's novel *Devil's Valley* (1998) is a piece of magical realism inspired by the true story of a small, isolated community hidden from the outside world in the remoteness of the Swartberg mountains. The valley is popularly known as Die Hel (The Hell), but its former residents prefer the official name, Gamkaskloof, which is derived from the Khoekhoen word for 'lion'.

The tiny settlement in the *kloof* (or narrow valley) was founded when a small group split off from a larger party of what were known as *trekboers* (the migrating farmers and herdsmen who were part of a general movement of mainly Dutch settlers into the interior before the Great Trek). This splinter group, consisting of the Mostert, Marais, Nel, Cordier and Swanepoel families, found the hidden valley when livestock strayed into a gorge along the Gamka River.

For many decades the group lived in almost total seclusion, until a rough road was built into the valley in the 1960s (although a donkey train had been making its way, every few months, through the area to Prince Albert since the early years of the century). A school was built in 1904 (finally closed in 1980), and the minister of the Dutch Reformed church of Prince Albert did make house calls in the valley. Even the tax collector found his way there, although he was famously rebuffed by the residents. The soil is fertile, and the residents kept livestock, grew vegetables, fruit, wheat, rye and tobacco, and foraged for honeybush and wild honey.

Strange community

Gamkaskloof featured in literature long before André Brink's novel. Boer leader Deneys Reitz tells of a brief visit to the valley, during his guerilla operations in the Anglo-Boer (South African) War, in the classic book *Commando*. He writes of his huge surprise in finding here 'a white man named Cordier, who lived there with his wife and a brood of half-wild children, in complete isolation from the outside world'. He expresses his gratitude for 'uncouth but sincere hospitality'.

Devil's Valley (published initially as *Duiwelskloof* in Afrikaans) tells a compelling story of a Cape Town crime reporter, Flip Lochner, who is drawn to the place after a brief encounter with one of its few residents who had made his way to the outside world. The reporter struggles to make sense of this lost world, whose inbred residents are deeply pious but also decadent and vindictive. Flip Lochner finds himself caught in tangled webs of personal intrigue that cross the generations and the boundaries between the living and the dead. As he moves between dream and reality, he develops a dangerous obsession with a woman of the valley who has the mark of the Devil etched on her flesh.

Devil's Valley has not been well received by the former residents of the Kloof who now live in the farms and villages of the Little Karoo. They have taken exception to his accounts of intermarriage and incest, and to his stereotypical portrayal of the people of the valley as backward, cruel and superstitious, even though Brink has been at pains to point out that the book is simply an imaginative projection of what the community would have been like if they had lived for several hundred years in *total* isolation. The controversy does, nevertheless, raise many difficult questions for writers. Moreover, Brink was not the first to be fascinated by the mythology: as early as the 1940s popular magazines and newspapers featured overly sensational articles about the 'strange community' of The Hell, which attracted intrusive gawkers.

The kloof today

Today Gamkaskloof still attracts visitors in search of a somewhat weird world, but nothing remains of its original human landscape: the last of the old residents, Piet Swanepoel, left in 1991. *The Sunday Times Lifestyle* magazine has advised that 'instead of an isolated settlement of gibbering hermits and raving lunatics who slip in and out of each other's bedrooms and forever curse God and his creation, visitors find a valley remarkable only for its spectacular natural beauty'.

Gamkaskloof, which is now under the custodianship of Western Cape Nature Conservation, is accessed from the summit of the dramatic Swartberg Pass (one of the highest mountain passes in South Africa), approximately 20 km from Prince Albert and 52 km from Oudtshoorn. From near the summit a rough road takes off directly west for 37 km into the valley. The road can be negotiated by ordinary sedan but you'll need to be careful – at one point it drops dramatically through a number of hairpin bends some 1 000 m, and drivers may expect a few anxious moments.

The ravine-like valley itself stretches out for about 20 km, along which are scattered the houses that belonged to the original families. Some of these structures have been restored and now provide self-catering visitor accommodation. They have a simple charm, built of unbaked bricks, their rafters constructed of olive wood, their floors made of compacted earth smeared with cattle dung mixed with the resin of the *soetdoring* tree.

Towards the end of the long valley is the Gamkas River, which cuts an impressive gorge through the Swartberg. This is an unpredictable river – for most of the year its waters are still and stagnant, but it can burst into a raging torrent. Nearby are the offices of Cape Nature Conservation, and at the far west end of the valley is the notorious 'ladder', the alternative route into Gamkaskloof.

AND WHAT'S MORE...

Discover the world of the **Gamkaskloof***, its people – both real and imagined – and the extraordinary landscape that makes it so memorable that it forms the backdrop to some of South Africa's most acclaimed works of literature. For either bookings or further information, contact* **Cape Nature Conservation** *on (044) 802 5300, george@cnc.org.za, www.capenature.org.za*

On the city's Greenmarket Square is the Old Town House, which now holds the Michaelis Collection and stands as an impressive example of mid-18th-century urban architecture, with 'its proud three-arched portico, its gay green shutters against the white and yellow plasterwork, its exuberant moundings and fanlights and its quaint belfry the Old Town House, for all its modesty, is as endearing a little rococo building as any found in Europe'.

Many other splendid early buildings line Government Avenue, which flanks the Company's Gardens, which were established in 1652. Here we have the Victorian-era neo-Classical Houses of Parliament (1885); the Gothic-type St George's Cathedral (1834); the Great Synagogue (European Baroque,1905); the Georgian-style Bertram House (1840s), now a museum furnished in 19th-century English Regency fashion; Tuynhuis, the city office of the State President (1751); the grand South African National Gallery (1914) and South African Museum (1893); and the Slave Lodge, now a cultural history museum.

Also in the central area, at 35 Strand Street, is the **Koopmans-De Wet House** (1701), an elegant 18th-century neo-Classical town-house, which is now a period museum with a fine collection of furniture and porcelain. Less grand but equally attractive are the mosques and cottages of the **Bo-Kaap**, home to part of the Cape Muslim community, on the slopes of Signal Hill above Buitengracht Street. Cape Town's fashionable gay village, **De Waterkant**, on the edge of the Bo-Kaap (between Somerset and Waterkant streets), has many beautifully restored cottages once occupied by ex-slaves.

The wider area

Above the southern suburb of Rondebosch, on the slopes of Table Mountain just to the east of the central area, is the handsome campus of the **University of Cape Town**, which boasts one of the country's oldest structures: the summer house (the Belvedere), built by the Dutch East India Company on its Rustenburg estate. Higher up, below Devil's Peak, is the Doric-style Rhodes Memorial, designed by Sir Herbert Baker as a tribute to the arch-imperialist and Cape colonial premier Cecil John Rhodes; lower down is Mosterts Mill (1796), off Rhodes Drive, Mowbray, which is one of only two surviving Dutch windmills in the country; and Groote Schuur, the elegant Cape Dutch residence of many of South Africa's prime ministers and president.

Victorian-style architecture graces a number of the smaller outlying centres and small towns that skirt the city.

McGregor, in fact, is more or less a Victorian village, though its restored cottages have a distinctive Cape Dutch flavour. Also well preserved are the 19th-century buildings of **Stanford** along the south coast. Rather unusual is **Matjiesfontein**, a Victorian health resort in the Karoo, which has been preserved as a 'living museum'. Matjiesfontein was established in 1884 by a Scottish entrepreneur, James Douglas Logan, and reopened after restoration in 1970.

MAKING CONTACT

Old Town House
(Michaelis Collection)
(021) 481 3933;
South African Cultural
History Museum
(021) 461 8242;
University of Cape Town
(021) 650 9111;
Matjiesfontein Resort
(023) 561 3011

The later years

The Western Cape is less well known for its 20th-century architecture. The centre of Cape Town is, however, rich in **Art Deco**, the style most evident around Greenmarket Square and along Plein Street – see, for example, the Garden Court Hotel, Kimberley House, the Commercial Union building, the Sun Assurance building, the General Post Office, and the Old Mutual building.

These Art Deco treasures stand in contrast to the almost brutal architecture of the **Modern** period, exemplified by the Artscape (previously Nico Malan) theatre complex and other edifices on the Foreshore, a part of the city reclaimed from the ocean after the Second World War. For glitzy **Post-Modern** architecture visit the Century City commercial centre and the Canal Walk shopping mall to the northeast of the city.

Rather more meaningful are buildings that have combined contemporary themes with traditional idioms, among them the Gugu S'Thebe arts, culture, and heritage village on the corner of Main and Church streets in the township of Langa, and the Philippi 'community facility precinct and public plaza' near the busy Philippi railway station on the Cape Flats.

A very different sort of architecture is to be found in the shack settlements of the Cape Flats. Taweni Gondwe's book *Shack Chic* (Quivertree Publications) breaks convention by celebrating the architecture of the humble squatter dwelling.

For contemporary 'green architecture' see the Tsala Treetop Lodge near Knysna, which is built into the canopy of the indigenous Knysna forest using the idiom of an ancient African ruin.

AND WHAT'S MORE...

South Africa has a considerable Art Deco heritage dating back to mainly to the 1930s. Johannesburg has about 100 Art Deco buildings in its central area, while the city of Springs is believed to have the largest number of small-scale Art Deco buildings in the world after Miami, USA. Durban is also regarded as one of the world's top Art Deco destinations, as is Cape Town, which recently hosted the World Congress on Art Deco. For more information, contact Barbara Spencer at the **Cape Art Deco Club** *on (021) 671 8150.*

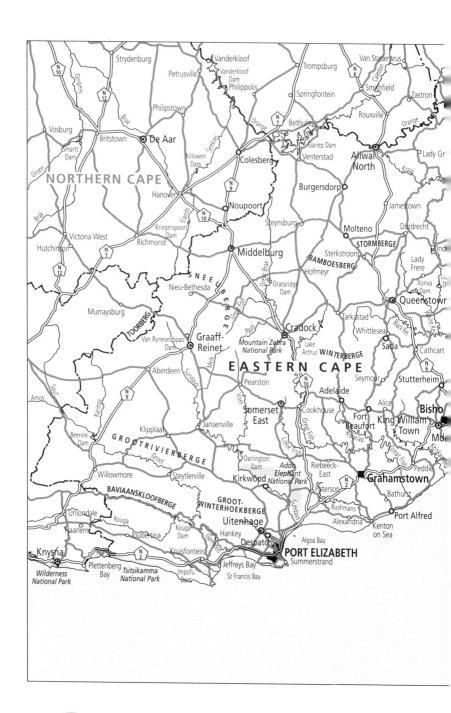

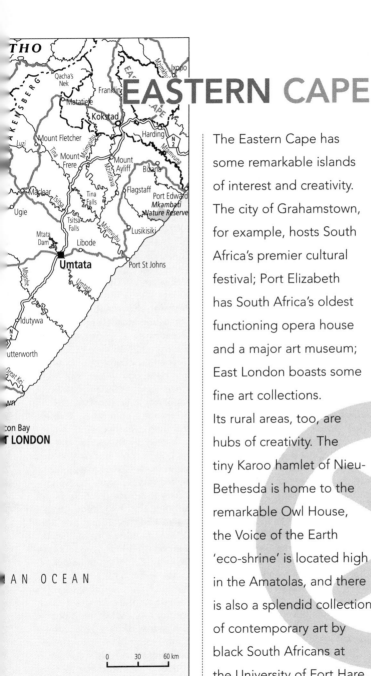

EASTERN CAPE

The Eastern Cape has some remarkable islands of interest and creativity. The city of Grahamstown, for example, hosts South Africa's premier cultural festival; Port Elizabeth has South Africa's oldest functioning opera house and a major art museum; East London boasts some fine art collections.

Its rural areas, too, are hubs of creativity. The tiny Karoo hamlet of Nieu-Bethesda is home to the remarkable Owl House, the Voice of the Earth 'eco-shrine' is located high in the Amatolas, and there is also a splendid collection of contemporary art by black South Africans at the University of Fort Hare.

eastern cape

Kaya Lendaba
(042) 203 1092 ,
www.shamwari.com;
Tsitsikamma
Khoisan Village
(042) 281 1450,
www.tsitsikamma.org.za;
Port St Johns
Tourism Information
(047) 564 1187,
www.ruraltourism.org.za;
De Beers Centenary
Art Gallery *(University*
of Fort Hare)
(040) 602 2011;
Nelson Mandela
Metropolitan Museum
(041) 586 1030

AFRICAN HERITAGE

The province is home to distinct groupings of the Xhosa, among them the amaPondo, the Thembu and the Gcaleka, who belong to the broader Nguni culture and thus have certain similarities to the Zulu, though many of their customs are unique (initiation, smoking long pipes, and smearing their bodies with a red ochre). Many traditions have disappeared beneath the burdens of colonialism and apartheid, but much has also survived, especially in rural areas.

Kaya Lendaba, in the Shamwari private game reserve north of Port Elizabeth is an African spiritual centre. It was built by mystic Credo Mutwa and offers spiritual therapy and the opportunity to study traditional health practices.

The **Tsitsikamma Khoisan** village near the Bloukrans River bridge along the Garden Route is South Africa's only cultural hub to feature the customs of South Africa's earliest peoples, and is dedicated to the welfare of the Khoisan people who remain within the region. For the most part, the village is given over to a crafts centre but does have traditional Khoekhoe huts on display. Accommodation is available on site.

There are plans to establish other cultural villages in the region, including the **Cwebeni** near Port St Johns on the Wild Coast which, at the time of writing (2004), was a well advanced project. It is being built with the government's poverty alleviation funds. It will also showcase Xhosa culture, and provide overnight accommodation. For an update, contact Port St Johns Tourism Information.

THE VISUAL ARTS

The historic campus of the **University of Fort Hare** in Alice hosts the De Beers Centenary Art Gallery, which holds one of South Africa's finest collections of work by contemporary black artists (including Gerard Sekota, Gerhard Bhengu, Selby Mvusi, and Port Elizabeth-born George Pemba), with an important ethnographic collection. The contemporary art goes back to the 1960s, when the head of African studies at the university, Professor EJ de Jager, and curator of the FS Malan Collection, Vincent Gitywa, recognised that black South African art was under threat.

Premier showcase

The **Nelson Mandela Metropolitan Museum** (the King George VI Art Gallery) on Park Drive, Port Elizabeth, is a contemporary showcase boasting collections of South African (and, especially, Eastern Cape) art, some British pieces, international printmaking displays, and Qing dynasty Oriental art.

Initially, there was resistance to the purchase of South African art, but in the 1960s the celebrated Walter Battiss persuaded the gallery to include paintings by such artists as Irma Stern, Alexis Preller, Gregoire Boonzaaier and Sidney Goldblatt. One of the most significant works is Dorothy Moss Kay's *The Eye of the Beholder*.

Today, the gallery focuses mainly on Eastern Cape works. Pieces from the permanent collection are rotated, but items not on display may be seen by appointment. The museum also stages exhibitions that have included work by Trevor Makhoba, William Kentridge and Sue Williamson.

East London

The **Vincent Gallery** at 2 Donald Street has works by leading South African artists, including Pierneef, Tinus de Jongh, Father Claerhout, Gregoire Bonzaaier, William Kentridge and Cecil Skotnes, who was born in East London. The **Ann Bryant Art Gallery** at 9 St Marks Road, Southernwood, offers an array of South African painting, sculptures, ceramics, and photography from the 1880s.

The country towns

The **Hester Rupert Art Museum** in Graaff-Reinet's Old Dutch Reformed church is devoted mainly to the art of the 1960s, with pieces by Walter Battiss, Gregoire Boonzaaier and Edoardo Villa. Also in Graaff-Reinet (in the Old Library Museum) is the Rembrandt van Rijn rock-art exhibition.

Walter Battiss was born in Somerset East and some of his work is on display in his home town's **Walter Battiss Art Gallery**, in the museum in Beaufort Street. Battiss was much influenced by the region's rock art, which is especially plentiful in the Stormberg and Drakensberg foothills.

The town of **Lady Grey** in the Witteberg mountains is the unlikely home of one of the country's three art colleges. A teacher at the Lady Grey Arts Academy suggested that 'the school is like finding a Broadway theatre in the middle of the Sahara'. Art Explore offers retreats in a mountain setting.

High in the Amatola mountains, near the village of Hogsback, is an unusual example of spiritual art: Diane Graham's **Voice of the Earth** 'eco-shrine'. The shrine, with its evocative mosaics, sculptures and paintings, celebrates 'the divine in nature'. In the equally small town of Alexandria, about 100 km from Port Elizabeth, is another restful place, the **Quin Sculpture Garden and Gallery**, which features the work of artist Maureen Quin.

The most unusual art in small-town Eastern Cape is, however, the **Owl House** in Nieu-Bethesda (see pages 50–51).

STAGE AND SCREEN

The Eastern Cape was home to one of South Africa's leading playwrights, **Athol Fugard**, who has produced some of his best plays in and around Port Elizabeth.

Port Elizabeth is home to the Victorian-style Opera House in Whites Street, the country's oldest functional opera venue. Upstairs is The Barn, an intimate space for local theatre productions. The city also boasts the historic, lavishly restored Feathermarket Hall, in Baaken Road, and its 1 000-seat auditorium.

The home of the performing arts in **East London** is the respected and long-established Guild Theatre in Selborne. There is, however, also the Orient Theatre off the Esplanade, which for the most part has served the black community, providing the space for such activities including jazz concerts, boxing promotions and political gatherings. The city also has an Arts Theatre (bookings through the Guild Theatre).

There is of course an abundance of theatre in **Grahamstown** during the National Arts Festival (see page 53). Major venues are the Rhodes University Theatre in Somerset Street, and the Monument Theatre in the Monument building.

MAKING CONTACT

FINE ART
Vincent Gallery
(043) 726 4356;
Ann Bryant Art Gallery
(043) 722 4044;
Hester Rupert
Art Museum
(049) 892 2121;
Rembrandt van Rijn
Rock-Art Exhibition
(Old Library Museum)
(049) 892 3801;
Walter Battiss Art Gallery
(042) 243 2079;
Art Explore
(051) 603 0261;
Voice of the Earth
Eco-shrine *(045) 962 1136,*
www.ecoshrine.co.za;
Quin Sculpture
Garden and Gallery
(046) 653 0121

THEATRE
The Barn
(041) 586 2256;
Feathermarket Hall
(041) 585 5514;
Guild Theatre
(043) 743 0704;
Orient Theatre
(043) 705 2902;
Guild Theatre
(043) 743 0704;
Rhodes University
Theatre *(046) 603 6111;*
Monument Theatre
(046) 622 7115

THEATRE
Stutterheim Amateur
Dramatics Society *(SADS)*
(043) 683 1465;
Kings Theatre
(043) 642 4397;
John Rupert Little
Theatre *(049) 892 6059;*
Lady Grey Arts Academy
(051) 603 0086

MUSIC & DANCE
International Library
of African Music
(Rhodes University)
(046) 603 8557/8547;
African Musical
Instruments Workshop
(046) 622 6252,
www.kalimba.co.za;
Emzini Jazz Café
(043) 726 9169;
Ekhaya Jazz Café
(041) 586 115;
Joy of Jazz
www.joyofjazz.co.za;
Schools Festival *www.*
schoolfest.foundation.org.za;
FNB Vita Dance Umdudo
(046) 622 3897,
www.artslink.co.za/fnb;
Amahlati Arts, Culture
and Development Festival
(043) 683 2024,
www.manderson.co.za;
Hogsback Spring Festival
(045) 962 1174

The smaller centres

There's is a fully-fledged theatre in Stutterheim, a venue that has served the local amateur dramatics society (SADS) since 1919; King William's Town has its Kings Theatre, Graaff-Reinet the John Rupert Little Theatre in Parsonage Street. Lady Grey offers a special surprise – each year the local Arts Academy here presents a three-day Passion Play.

SOUNDS OF MUSIC

Grahamstown's **International Library of African Music**, on Rhodes University's main campus, has a magnificent collection of recordings, videos, books and instruments. It was founded by Professor Andrew Tracey, who was presented with the Premier's Award in 2002 for lifetime achievement. Also in Grahamstown is **African Musical Instruments**, a workshop established by Andrew Tracey's father, Hugh, and a magnet for musicians from across the world. Here, visitors can watch the drums, marimbas, kalimbas and other traditional instruments being made and played.

Jazz from the sticks

The cities and townships of the Eastern Cape are famed for their lively music. In the 1950s **Queenstown**, for example, was known as 'Little Jazz Town', a place where such dixieland bands as the Darktown Negroes and Meekly Matshikiza's Big Four entertained in drinking halls that would fill with miners when the trains to Johannesburg made their overnight stops. One of the earliest female jazz bands in South Africa was the Queenstown

Gay Glamour Girls, while jazz great Todd Matshikiza went to school in the town.

Today the best jazz in the Eastern Cape is to be heard in the pubs and restaurants around East London and Port Elizabeth. The clubs and shebeens (drinking dens) of the sprawling township of **Mdantsane**, on the edge of East London, are alive with music. Notable is the Emzini African Restaurant and Jazz Café, now located in the craft market area of Hemingways Casino. Recommended in Port Elizabeth is Ekhaya African Jazz at the corner of Whites and Belmont streets.

The province's annual **jazz festivals** are all sponsored by Standard Bank Joy of Jazz. Grahamstown is host to the National Youth Jazz Festival (June), Joy of Jazz (beginning of July), and the jazz festival during the National Arts Festival in the first two weeks of July. The Eastern Cape Jazz Manyano is held in East London.

EVENTS

As we've noted, the Eastern Cape is home to South Africa's premier cultural celebration, the **National Arts Festival** held in Grahams-town in early July (*see page 53*). Apart from the three jazz festivals mentioned above, the city also hosts a number of youth and specialist events during the year, including the **FNB Vita Dance Umdudo** (in April), a celebration of contemporary choreography.

A few of the smaller provincial towns stage annual cultural shows, among them Stutterheim with its Amahlati Arts, Culture and Development Festival and Hogsback with its Spring Festival.

THE PRINTED WORD

The Eastern Cape is immensely rich in its literary associations, to which you'll find excellent introductions in the **National English Literary Museum** at 87 Beaufort Street, Grahamstown. The Eastern Cape boasts some of the country's greatest novelists, playwrights and poets, among them Olive Schreiner, Thomas Pringle, Guy Butler, John Tengo Jabavu, Tiyo Soga, JM Coetzee, André Brink, Zakes Mda and, surprisingly, Nelson Mandela (who has added literary merit to his many other distinctions).

The Eastern Cape's top early writer is undoubtedly **Olive Schreiner**, author of *From Man to Man*, *Undine*, and the internationally acclaimed *The Story of an African Farm*, which was first published in 1883 and is now recognised as the first major novel to come out of Africa. Schreiner was born at the Wesleyan mission station at Wittebergen near Herschel, and when she was six years old moved with her family to the mission at Healdtown, 10 km from Fort Beaufort (where Mandela was later to study). Schreiner wrote that 'my childhood was so bitter and dark, but I cling to the memories of it and especially the places I lived at. They were so unutterably lovely and it was in nature I found all the joy and help I had in those lonely years'.

When Olive was 12 her parents separated, and her father was declared bankrupt. She moved with her siblings to Cradock which, more than any other place, is associated with her memory. The Schreiner house at 9 Cross Street, where the Schreiner children lived for three years, is now a branch of the English Language Literary Museum.

Olive left Cradock at the age of 15 to work as a governess on a farm near Barkly East. In later years, however, she was to return to the district, to work as a governess on the farms Klein Gannahoek and Ratelhoek. It was the desolate but beautiful Karoo landscapes of these farms that inspired some of her greatest work. *The Story of an African Farm* begins with an evocative description of Klein Gannahoek, and the *kopje* to which she refers can still be seen on the farm, but the homestead she goes on to describe is now in ruins.

Schreiner was to marry a local man, Samuel Cron Cronwright from the farm Kranzplaas, and was eventually to be buried in the district. Her grave, a rounded sarcophagus on the summit of Buffelskop (on the farm Buffelshoek, 24 km south of Cradock on the Mortimer road), is one of the most remarkable burial sites in South Africa. Olive had initially been laid to rest in the family plot in Maitland cemetery in Cape Town but her body was exhumed and reinterred on the mountain top, together with those of her husband, her long-dead baby, and her dog.

A number of acclaimed writers, including Roy Campbell, Guy Butler, and Stephen Gray, have made real and imaginary pilgrimages up Buffelskop and have written of the gravesite. The large white bird that soared above the hilltop at the moment of her reburial features in Roy Campbell's poem, *Buffel's Kop*.

AND WHAT'S MORE...

Visit Olive Schreiner's grave for yourself! Arrangements can be made to visit the hilltop tomb, but be advised that you'll need to be reasonably fit. The climb up the mountain takes about one hour. Contact the **Schreiner Museum** *to secure a key to the gate on the farm. Note that the access road to the base of Buffelskop is in poor condition; a 4x4 or 'bakkie' would be an advantage. Contact the* **Schreiner Museum** *on (048) 881 5251; for additional information, call the* **National English Literary Museum** *on (046) 622 7042.*

The barren landscape of the Karoo has inspired great creative impulse. Apart from Helen Martins' Owl House, there is, for example, Olive Schreiner's Story of an African Farm, Athol Fugard's Road to Mecca, and David Kramer's musical Karoo Kitaar Blues. Other authors and artists with strong associations with the Karoo include Pauline Smith, CJ Langenhoven, Walter Battiss, Dan Jacobson, Guy Butler and Anthony Sher.

The fantasy world of the Owl House

'The Road to my Mecca was one I had to travel alone. It was a journey on which no one could keep me company, and because of that, now it is over, there is only me there at the end of it...' (Words spoken by the character representing Helen Martins in the film *The Road to Mecca*.)

Nieu-Bethesda is hidden in the Gat River valley beneath the Sneeuberg mountains, a surprising oasis in the barrenness of the Karoo, and it seems to have a rare spiritual quality that activates artistic genius. The village is most famously associated with Helen Martins, the creator of the extraordinary Owl House.

Helen Martins (or Miss Helen as she was known in the village) transformed her cottage into a bizarre fantasy world of cement sculptures, mirrors and glittering glass. She worked compulsively, along with the assistance of her manservant Koos Malgas, for a period of 12 years. She created hundreds of sculptures.

Helen Martins is South Africa's best-known example of an 'outsider artist'. The value and significance of outsider art (or 'art brut') was first recognised by the French artist Jean Dubuffet, who described it as 'fantastic, raw, visionary art created by individuals often maladjusted, with no art training, who work outside the mainstream of the art world'. Outsider art is created on the fringes of society, and is a form of 'private theatre' performed by individuals who seem to care very little for the opinions of those around them. At the time of its creation the art is invariably considered ridiculous or outlandish, or perhaps even a threat to social values, but in later years it may provoke some interest and even acclaim.

Other so-called outsider artists in South Africa include Nukain Mabusa, who created a fantasy garden of geometric patterns on a hillslope at Revolver Creek near Barberton; Jackson Hlungwani, whose New Jerusalem is discussed elsewhere, and Ron van Zyl, who created a religious sculpture garden on a hill close to Echo Caves near Ohrigstad in Mpumalanga. Helen Martins and Nukain Mabusa are among 44 others internationally listed in John Maizel's book, *Raw Creation: Outsider Art and Beyond*.

Miss Helen's tragic life

Unhappily, the Owl House speaks not only of an unusual creative talent but also of personal anguish: Helen Martins was a tortured woman, rejected by the community. She was born in Nieu-Bethesda in December 1897, the youngest of six children, and studied in Graaff-Reinet to be a teacher. She had a short, unsuccessful marriage, and spent almost 20 years caring for her ailing parents. In 1945 her father died, leaving her alone and bereaved. Over the following years Helen Martins became reclusive, eccentric and isolated from an increasingly suspicious local community.

In about 1964 Miss Helen employed Koos Malgas, an itinerant sheepshearer, to help her make cement-and-glass statues, and he became her only friend and companion. In August 1976 she committed suicide by swallowing caustic soda. She took her life because she could not bear the thought of going blind – the great theme of her life and work was light, and the idea of perpetual darkness was unthinkable.

Koos Malgas stayed on for two years before moving to Worcester, but in 1991 he returned to the Miss Helen's Owl House to assist in its restoration. By then, the property had been declared a national monument and the Owl House Foundation had been established. Malgas died in November 2000.

The story of Miss Helen and her Owl House came to the public attention through Athol Fugard's play *The Road to Mecca*, and the film based on it. Athol and his wife Sheila, whose literary work has also been inspired by Nieu-Bethesda, have a cottage in the village and spend part of the year there.

Showcase of the bizarre

The place is open to the public. Around the cottage is the Camel Yard, a cluttered kaleidoscope of cement sculptures that include figures of some of Miss Helen's favourite creatures – owls and camels – as well as of monsters, towers and churches, pyramids, sun-worshippers, and pilgrims. The sculptures link the Christian West with Eastern ideas and philosophy (Miss Helen was inspired by both the Bible and the writings of Omar Khayyam).

One of the major tableaus in the Yard, which greatly angered the deeply religious villagers of Nieu-Bethesda, is a procession of shepherds and wise men heading *towards* the East (instead of, that is, from the East towards Bethlehem).

The interior of the house is all sparkle and glitter, full of ornaments and figurines, candles and mirrors, the walls are covered with crushed glass of different colours – a fantastical, bizarre home, rich in symbolism. In the Honeymoon Room, for example, there is a red sun in the window with green eyes representing the jealousy of love. There are also two beds, instead of the single honeymoon bed that might be expected, perhaps indicating Miss Helen's own sad experience with love.

Spinoffs for the village

The legacy of Helen Martins has provided a huge boost to the lagging fortunes of Nieu Bethesda. Once a prosperous centre for the local farming district, it was in sharp decline by the 1950s. Isolated among the Sneeuberg mountains, it became home to a poor and increasingly marginal white and coloured community. Today, however, the Owl House brings almost 15 000 visitors to the town each year, and there are at least 16 guesthouses, a small backpackers' establishment, two restaurants, a coffee shop, a pub, and two art galleries. However, despite its great benefit to the town, the Owl House still provokes strong feelings in certain individuals and, in July 2003, a number of the statues were vandalised.

AND WHAT'S MORE...

For further information on Miss Helen Martins and her unusual home, contact the **Owl House** *on (0490) 841 1642, owlhouse@global.co.za, www.owlhouse.co.za; or call the* **Friends of the Owl House** *on (049) 8410 1733. There are a number of published guidebooks available, including Anne Emslie's* The Owl House *(Penguin).*

eastern cape

The power of the Karoo

Many a writer has been inspired by the harsh beauty of the Great Karoo. **Guy Butler**, long-time professor of English at Rhodes University in Grahamstown, wrote of its great sunlit spaces in poetry and books spanning a period of more than half a century; among his major titles were the autobiographical *Karoo Morning* (1977), *Bursting World* (1983), and *A Local Habitation* (1991). His *Karoo Morning* tells of his childhood in Cradock, where he was born in 1918. The Butler family home, The Poplars, was on the corner of Bree and Church streets but was demolished after flood damage; the house in which he his wife Jean lived for 50 years, known as High Corner, is at the top of High Street in Grahamstown.

Among other works set in the sunlit interior are the contemporary novels of **Etienne van Heerden**, among them *Kikuyu*, a piece of magic realism that brings together the real sights and experiences of the Karoo with a fantasy world; *The Diary of Iris Vaughan*, which provides a child's eye view of Cradock and other towns in the Karoo; **Eve Palmer**'s classic *The Plains of Cambedoo* (1966), set on the farm Cranemere and a compelling exploration of the many different aspects of Karoo life and landscape; the contemporary writing of Sterkstroom-born **Farida Karodia** (*Daughters of Twilight*, 1986; *Vlenterhoek*, 2002), and **André Brink**'s *Rumours of Rain* (1978), which is set on a farm between Cathcart and Stutterheim. The dramatic landscapes

of the Stormberg mountains also had a huge influence on the internationally noted **William Plomer**, who lived on the farm Marsh Moor (25 km northeast of Molteno) with family friends during 1921.

Then there is the Little Karoo hamlet of Nieu Bethesda, with its Owl House, inspiration for **Athol Fugard**'s plays *A Road to Mecca* (see page 50–51) and *A Valley Song*. His wife, **Sheila Fugard**, was author of *A Revolutionary Woman*, which brings together the real and the mythical in a village she names New Kimberley but which is clearly based on Nieu-Bethesda.

PE roots

Athol Fugard, however, is more closely associated with **Port Elizabeth** where, although born in Middelburg, he grew up. His 1994 autobiography, *Cousins*, refers to the memories of his youth, to places where he lived and studied (Marist Brothers College and Port Elizabeth Technical College), and to places that provided him with the memories that shaped his writings, among them the St George's Park tearoom, which his mother ran for 30 years.

A number of Fugard plays are set in and around the city. *The Blood Knot*, for example, takes place in the poor, grimy settlement of Korsten, while the background for his acclaimed *Boesman and Lena* is the Swartkops mudflats, and the park tearoom the setting for *'Master Harold'... and the Boys*. Many of his other plays make reference to New Brighton township, where he worked in the company of black playwrights John Kani and Winston Ntshona.

AND WHAT'S MORE...

Writer **Etienne van Heerden**, *a master of magical realism, came to international attention with his* Ancestral Voices *(1989). This was followed by* Leap Year *(1997)*, Kikuyu *(1998) and* The Long Silence of Mario Salviati *(2003). Van Heerden grew up in the Karoo, on the family farm Doornbosch between the towns of Graaff-Reinet and Murraysburg, and is currently professor at the University of Cape Town. For more information on this acclaimed author, visit the website www. etiennevanheerden.co.za*

Grahamstown: the premier celebration

Once a year, for eleven days in July, Grahamstown is transformed into South Africa's Festival City.

The occasion began in 1974 as a celebration of English culture. In some senses Grahamstown still resembles a 19th-century English cathedral city, but by the early 1980s the festival had begun to shed its 'colonial' ethos, although it was still criticised for its apparent isolation from the political struggle and turmoil of the time. It was only really after 1994 that the organisers truly reached out to the multiplicity of cultures in South Africa. Then, again, its linguistic medium has remained almost exclusively English.

Post-freedom problems

In its first year it featured just 60 shows and attracted a few hundred visitors. By 2002 there were more than 600 events on the main and fringe programmes, and more than 100 000 visitors. It had become South Africa's most important space for creative expression; many of the trends and ideas that emerged at the festival spread across the country.

Ironically, however, as the festival expanded and became more inclusive (especially after political transition in the mid-1990s) so it faced a significant crisis of funding and image. Arts commentator Mike van Graan wrote of this in *City Life* magazine (June 2002):

'Post '94 more and more black practitioners were encouraged to take part in the festival, but no-one went to see them, because the audiences were still white ... So you had a huge contradiction in that you have these mainly white audiences, but what the festival was offering them was more diverse. The market became unsustainable.'

The problem was highlighted by the emergence of many other large and contrasting festivals nationwide, occasions such as Arts Alive in Johannesburg, the Cape Town Festival, Awesome Africa in Durban, and Oudtshoorn's Klein Karoo Nasionale Kunstefees. In 2001, Standard Bank brought the problems to a head when it pulled out as main sponsor, indicating its intention to support other festivals across the country, especially those related to jazz. Provincial government and the National Arts Council provided emergency funding to ensure the Grahamstown's show continued, but there has been downscaling. For some, the magic is gone (though for others there is now a new sense of expectancy).

Close links

The so-called and now perhaps inappropriately named 'Settler Country' (named after the 1820 British settlers) has important associations with a number of 19th- and 20th-century English writers. **Thomas Pringle**, who was born in the Scottish border region, arrived in South Africa with a settler party and was granted land in the Baviaans Valley, at the foot of the Winterberg. A number of his poems make reference to the valley settlement known as Glen

AND WHAT'S MORE...

Long hailed as the country's premier showcase for the arts, the **National Festival of the Arts** *in Grahamstown is the biggest and most spectacular of South Africa's cultural festivities (although a number of 'smaller' festivals are indeed catching up at a rapid pace – all the better for the local arts scene!). To contact the festival organisers, call (046) 603 1103, info@nafest.co.za, www.nafest.co.za; for accommodation during the festival period, e-mail booking@ grahamstownaccom.co.za or visit the website www. grahamstownaccom.co.za; ticket bookings for performances can be made through Computicket, www. computicket.co.za; the festival is usually held from 29 June to 6 July but this varies from year to year.*

AND WHAT'S MORE...

Venture into the land
that helped fuel the fine
imagination and eloquent
words of one of South
Africa's finest novelists,
the famed Sir Percy
Fitzpatrick, most famous
as the author of the
timeless Jock of the
Bushveld classic. Visit
his farm **Amanzi** (or
'Balmoral', as Sir Percy
would have known it),
(042) 233 0425,
or contact the
Percy Fitzpatrick Library
(042) 233 0353 for more
information of this
talented writer.

Lynden (which is near the village of Bedford). The gravel road that follows the valley takes you to many places linked to this important early poet: the stone church where he is buried; the Eildon farmstead, which still belongs to the Pringle family; the Bushman cave referred to in Pringle's poetry; the witgat tree under which he composed some of his lines, and the site of the first settler camp, which is marked by a cairn. A contemporary author, **Marguerite Poland**, has also adopted the Baviaans Valley as the setting for her work. Although she uses fictional names in reference to farms and other landmarks in her *Train to Doringbult* (1987) the descriptions refer, unmistakably, to the valley.

About 20 km from Grahamstown is the settler village of **Salem**, close to where Nobel Prize laureate **JM Coetzee** set part of his 1999 novel *Disgrace*. It was to a sprawling farmhouse on an untidy smallholding outside Salem that the novel's professor retreated after being accused of harassing a female student, and it was on this smallholding that a series of deeply disturbing events unfolded, which provide a metaphor of the deep-seated anxieties in post-apartheid society.

Also associated with the Eastern Cape is **Sir Percy Fitzpatrick** of *Jock of the Bushveld* fame, who was born in King William's Town and schooled at St Aidan's College in Grahamstown. He is strongly connected with Coega and the Sundays River valley, where he spent 18 years of his life. The farm owned by Fitzpatrick, called Amanzi (originally named 'Balmoral'), is along the Coega

River and embraces a gracious old homestead with a wide veranda, but may only be visited by appointment. Near the village of Addo is the Percy Fitzpatrick Library and its commemorative plaque.

Xhosa creativity

The Eastern Cape, with a tradition of liberal mission education, was the region that gave birth to the first written literature produced by black South Africans.

The area in which Thomas Pringle lived and wrote was also home to **Ntsikana**, the first Xhosa poet to have his work written down and translated into English. Ntsikana was born at Qakeni in the Amatola mountains and buried at Thathwa in the Winterberg.

The focal point of black South African literature was the two great educational institutions in the little town of Alice – **Fort Hare University** and **Lovedale College** (site of the Lovedale Mission Press). Some of the literary figures connected with these two institutions include JK Bokwe, JJR Bolobe, Basil Somhlahlo, John Tengo Jabavu, and Noni Jabavu.

The village of **Mgwali**, about 25 km from Stutterheim on the road to Tsomo, is closely linked to the memory of **Tiyo Soga**, the greatest of the early Xhosa writers. Soga was the first black African to be trained overseas. He was a pupil at Lovedale College, but left during the War of the Axe in 1846. Ordained as a Presbyterian minister in Scotland, he returned to the Eastern Cape as a missionary in 1857 and was placed in charge of the church at Mgwali (which can still be visited).

Soga translated part of John Bunyan's *Pilgrim's Progress* into Xhosa, and in 1993 a number of his articles, which first appeared in the *Indaba*, were published as the *The Journal and Selected Writings of the Reverend Tiyo Soga*. Mgwali is now a popular destination for travellers: it offers a range of traditional cultural activities and basic accommodation (contact Ingrid, Ncamiso or Connie).

The Xhosa writer best known in the first part of the twentieth century was **Samuel Mqhayi**, who spent 20 years living on the hill called Ntambozuko ('Hill of Glory'), which is just off the old road between King William's Town and East London and near the town of Berlin. A tall memorial column marks his burial site.

Tragic figures

One of the most important of the contemporary black novelists from the Eastern Cape is **Zakes Mda**. Mda's novel *The Heart of Redness* (2000) is set at Qolora Mouth on the Transkei Wild Coast and tells the story of Nongqawuse, the prophetess whose visions of an ancestor's spirit led to what became known as the 'cattle killing movement', a tragic episode that led to famine and the death of more than 40 000 Xhosa people. Mda provides an interpretation of events that is highly sympathetic to Nongqawuse. This traumatic historical event was also the inspiration for a number of earlier works, among them HIE Dhlomo's play *The Girl who Killed to Save* (1935), and AC Jordan's *The Wrath of the Ancestors* (1980).

At least two key political figures, who are also authors, have strong associations with the Eastern Cape. The Black Consciousness leader **Steve Biko**, who was born in Ginsberg, King William's Town, penned the angry polemic *I Write What I Like* (1978). His life was the subject of Donald Wood's biography *Biko* (1978) and Richard Attenborough's film *Cry Freedom* (1983). **Nelson Mandela** is, of course, the author of the weighty autobiography *Long Walk to Freedom* (1994), which features many places in the region connected with his childhood and education (see the companion volume *South Africa's Top Sites – Struggle*).

ARCHITECTURE

Traditional Xhosa dwellings can still be seen in the remoter parts of the Transkei region. Those more interested **vernacular settler** architecture, which drew its ideas from early 19th-century England, should visit the area around **Grahamstown** and such small towns as Salem and Bathurst.

The most important provincial town in architectural terms is probably **Graaff-Reinet** (although Grahamstown competes well), which has excellent examples of various styles but perhaps most notably Victorian Cape Dutch. Here, more than 200 houses have been restored to their original form and condition and are proclaimed national monuments. **Karoo** towns such as Pearston, Cradock, and Nieu-Bethesda are also significant for their graceful Karoo cottage architecture.

Among the area's interesting contemporary buildings (and a possible place to stay) is the prize-winning, eclectic and futuristic Stratford's Guesthouse at 68 Frere Road, Vincent, East London.

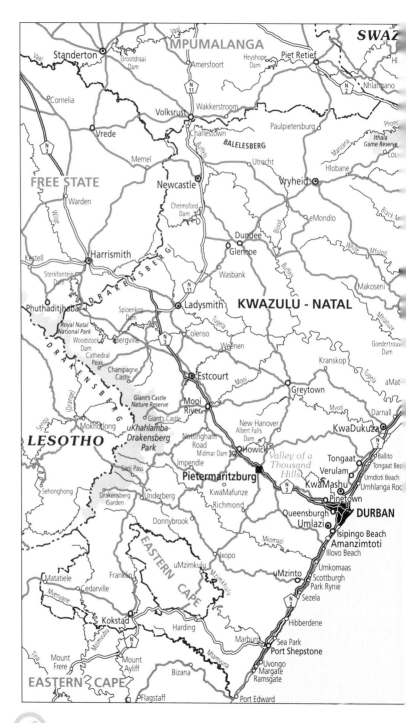

KWAZULU-NATAL

Durban is is home to, among much else, the Durban Art Museum's eccentric Red Eye @rt, the avant-garde BAT Centre, the NSA Gallery, a bevy of experimental theatre venues, and to the Awesome Africa festival. Elsewhere there are the highly praised Tatham Art Gallery (Pietermaritzburg); Rorke's Drift Art Centre, which has played such a crucial role in training black talent; the Ardmore Studios in the shadow of the 'Berg, and the Splashy Fen music festival. KwaZulu-Natal has strong associations with some of South Africa's best literary output, including Alan Paton's heart-wrenching *Cry, The Beloved Country*.

kwazulu-natal

Shakaland
(035) 460 0912,
res@shakaland.com,
www.shakaland.com;
Simunye
(035) 450 3111,
www.proteahotels.co.za;
Dumazulu
(035) 562 2260,
www.goodersonleisure.com;
Intibane
(032) 946 2941;
Kwabekitunga
(035) 460 0644;
Isibindi Zulu Lodge
(035) 474 1473,
www.zulunet.co.za;
Veyane
(035) 550 4325,
072 588 8290,
www.veyane.co.za;
Ilala Weavers
(035) 562 0630/1,
www.ilala.co.za;
Umgungundlovu
and Amafe
(035) 870 2050/1/2/3;
Utshwayelo
(Muzi) 073 135 8198

AFRICAN HERITAGE

One of the great attractions of this province is the Zulu cultural legacy. The nation was forged in the 1820s by the warrior king Shaka, who brought all the Nguni clans in the region together under his control. They were finally conquered by the British in the war of 1879, but the royal dynasty survived (the titular head today is Goodwill Zwelethini).

This world has since undergone dramatic transformation, but there are a number of cultural villages that provide insight into the Zulu lifestyle and customs of a bygone era (although, often, in very commercialised fashion).

Living museums

Shakaland, near Eshowe (off the R66, the road to Melmoth), is a four-star hotel complex (of the Protea Group) consisting of about 50 beehive huts with en-suite bathrooms. The village was built as the set for the television epic *Shaka Zulu*. Visitors are given a hands-on introduction to the Zulu social system and its history. There are also demonstrations of dance, basketry, bead-making, pottery, and spear- and shield-making, and a *sangoma* (traditional healer) is on hand for consultation.

About 10 km east of Melmoth is **Simunye** pioneer village. The lodge is built around a settler store in the Mfule River valley; the cultural experience provides a look at the relationship between Zulus and white settlers at the time of the Anglo-Zulu War of 1879.

Dumazulu ('thundering Zulu'), near Hluhluwe, is a good base from which to explore the game reserves. There are 23 luxury suites in huts, and a traditional village.

The Intibane Cultural Village on the **Intibane Game Ranch** enables visitors to combine wildlife and culture; **Kwabekitunga** is on Stewart's Farm near Eshowe; the luxury **Isibindi Zulu Lodge** near the Anglo-Zulu War battlefields of Isandlwana and Rorke's Drift is described as 'an architectural celebration of the Zulu'; **Veyane** on the edge of the Greater St Lucia Wetlands Park caters for budget travellers.

Other attractions

Ilala, near Hluhluwe, is one of the country's most successful craft projects – providing a living for some 2 000 locals, its products marketed worldwide. The crafters live in the village, where you'll see them engaged in basket-weaving, beading, carving, pot-making and other traditional activities.

Umgungundlovu, Dingane's capital near the Valley of the Kings, and **Ondini**, where King Cetshwayo established his royal residence (it was burnt to the ground by British invaders in 1879), have been restored. The latter is also the site of the **Amafa Heritage** showplace.

The far north of the province is home to the **Tsonga** people. This group has a distinctive lifestyle which, traditionally, has centred on the catching of fish in and around the vast, shallow lagoons of the area. It is a lifestyle very different from that of the Zulu, which was based on cattle. For the Tsonga experience stay overnight at the Utshwayelo Kosi Mouth camp site outside the northern entrance to the Kosi Bay coastal forest reserve; this is run as a development project by the kwaMvutshane community.

The **PheZulu Cultural Village**, with its dance performances, is in the Valley of a Thousand Hills; **Isithumba**, which features contemporary Zulu life, lies in the Umgeni valley; the **Ecabazini** Zulu cultural homestead is at Albert Falls Dam near Pietermaritzburg.

In the far south is the **KwaZulu-Natal Multicultural Village**, an initiative that hadn't been completed at the time of writing (2004).

THE VISUAL ARTS

The province's premier collection (more than 5 000 works) is housed in the **Durban Art Gallery** in City Hall on Smith Street. Opened in 1911, the core collection was established in 1920 with a donation of 400-plus pieces, among them excellent 17th-century Dutch and Flemish paintings and British, French and Dutch ceramics.

The gallery has also been accumulating traditional and contemporary local art, and a major theme since the 1990s has been the promotion of human rights.

The gallery has responded to the challenges that face art museums in contemporary South Africa, managing successfully to avoid the elitism tag through its outreach programmes and its popular, experimental presentation of artforms – and, in consequence, it's been pulling in over 200 000 visitors each year. Perhaps the most innovative of its initiatives is **Red Eye @rt**, an eccentric exposition of works, created in a variety of art forms, on the first Friday of every month. Founded by Suzy Bell as an attempt to enliven the local art scene, it includes experimental paintings, sculptures, performance, poetry, live music, dance and fashion.

Worth a visit, too, is the **Natal Society of Arts** (NSA) Gallery at 166 Bulwer Road, in Glenwood – a pleasant venue for lunches and teas, and where exhibitions of contemporary art are held. On site is an arts-and-crafts shop and a photographic centre.

For the African experience, however, visit the **Bartel Arts Trust (BAT) Centre** at the small-craft harbour off Durban's Victoria Embankment. Here, an avant garde multipurpose venue has been established in an old Navy hangout, now brightly decorated with African murals, where one can listen to jazz, take part in drumming circles (Tuesday nights) and poetry readings, and enjoy the work of the resident artists. The BAT Centre also houses the acclaimed Menzi Mchunu Gallery, the Bayside Gallery, the Democratic Art Gallery, the BAT Arts and Crafts Shop, and the Intensive Care Café.

For contemporary African arts and crafts, visit Durban's **Tourist Junction** at 160 Pine Street, home to the Africa Art Gallery. The famous **Campbell Collections**, at 220 Marriott Road, have one of South Africa's most significant ethnology displays. Also worth visiting is the 26-panelled 'Peace Quilt' at the **Durban International Convention Centre**, to which quilt-makers from 29 countries around the world have donated around 800 fabric squares, known as 'peace bricks' (each depicts a symbol of peace and is signed by the artist). Other city galleries include Art Routes Africa at 50 Florida Road, ArtSPACE at 3 Millar Road, Stamford Hill, the Durban Institute of Technology Gallery, and the Elizabeth Gordon Gallery.

MAKING CONTACT

AFRICAN HERITAGE
PheZulu Cultural Village
(031) 777 1000;
Isithumba
082 716 8997;
Ecabazini
(033) 342 1928;
KwaZulu-Natal
Multicultural Village
www.kzn.org.za;

GALLERIES
Durban Art Gallery
(031) 311 2262/5,
www.durban.gov.za/
museums/artgallery;
Natal Society of
Arts Gallery
(031) 202 3686,
www.nsagallery.co.za;
BAT Centre
(031) 332 0451,
www.batcentre.co.za;
Menzi Mchunu Gallery
(031) 332 0451;
Bayside Gallery
(031) 368 5547;
Democratic Art Gallery
(031) 332 0451;
BAT Arts and Crafts Shop
(031) 332 9951;
Durban Tourist Junction
(031) 366 7500;
Africa Art Gallery
(031) 304 7915;
Campbell Collections
(031) 207 3432,
www.khozi.und.ac.za;
Art Routes Africa
(031) 561 1515;
ArtSPACE
(031) 312 0793;
Durban Institute of
Technology Gallery
(031) 204 2207;
Elizabeth Gordon Gallery
(031) 303 8133

kwazulu-natal

MAKING CONTACT

Natal Museum
(033) 345 1404;
Tatham Art Gallery
(033) 342 1804,
bell@tatham.org.za;
Rorke's Drift Art Centre
(034) 642 1627/1805;
Rorke's Drift Lodge
(034) 642 1805;
Midlands Meander
(033) 330 8195, www.
midlandsmeander.co.za;
Misty Mountain Artists'
Retreat *(033) 263 6250;*
Boston–Bulwer Beat
(033) 234 1909,
http://bostonbulwerbeat.
kzn.org.za;
Southern Drakensberg–
Sani Saunter
(033) 701 1471,
www.sanisaunter.org.za;
Drakensberg Meander
(036) 468 1314;
Hilton Meander
(033) 343 1456,
083 420 8656;
Thousand Hills Experience
(031) 777 1874,
http://1000hills.kzn.org.za;
Southern Explorer
(039) 314 4951, www.
southernexplorer.co.za;
KwaZulu-Natal Tourism
www.kzn.org.za;
Ardmore *(036) 468 1242,*
www.ardmoreceramics.co.za

The second city

The provincial capital Pietermaritzburg (or Maritzburg, as it is fondly known) is also home to important art collections. The **Natal Museum** at 273 Loop Street has an extensive ethnological collection that includes important 19th-century Zulu carvings (most notable is Cetshwayo's chair). The **Tatham Art Gallery**, housed in the Old Supreme Court building in Commercial Road, opposite the City Hall, has a striking collection dating back to 1903. Despite its colonial origins, the gallery now houses some excellent contemporary African art, including Willie Bester's evocative sculpture *1913 Land Act* (a wooden bench with ball and chains), and David Koloane's *Moonlight and Roses*.

Art in the countryside

Many of rural areas and smaller provincial towns also contribute to the cultural scene. One of remotest venues has recently received much-deserved but belated recognition for its role in supporting art during the dark years of apartheid. The **Rorke's Drift Art Centre**, deep in the uThukela valley and famed as an Anglo-Zulu Way battlesite (1879), was once the only place where black artists could receive formal training in the visual arts. In the early 1960s the Church of Sweden Mission (Evangelical Lutheran) established the centre as a self-help project, and later introduced a certificate of art. Over the years, a number of graduates of the centre have made their mark in the art world. The noted contemporary artist Christine Lambert has a gallery not far away, at Rorke's Drift Lodge.

Art and craft routes

The **Midlands Meander**, a popular weekend excursion from Durban and Pietermaritzburg, extending from about Howick to Mooi River, has about 160 studios, workshops and outlets. The route now also takes in Mpophomeni (off the R617 outside Howick), a place once notorious for crime and violence but now the focus of a community tourism programme that includes art, crafts, traditional dancing and homestays. The Midlands, in fact, provides a lovely setting for art holidays, such as those offered at the **Misty Mountain Artists' Retreat** by painter Richard Rennie.

Among other routes are the **Boston–Bulwer Beat** along the R617 in the Southern 'Berg foothills; the **Southern Drakensberg–Sani Saunter**, further into the mountains; the **Drakensberg Meander** in the central 'Berg near Estcourt; the **Hilton Meander**, in and around the village of Hilton, above Maritzburg; the **Thousand Hills Experience**, around Botha's Hill, and the **Southern Explorer**, on the South Coast.

Many venues are small and geared to a market that is not always discriminating, but there are places of significance. The ceramics workshop of **Ardmore Art Studios** in the Champagne Valley is known for its idiosyncratic style, an idiom characterised by bold colour and elaborate design. The artists are from local rural communities, and have worked since 1985 under the ceramic artist Fée Halsted-Berning. Artists include Bonnie Ntshalintshali (who died aged 32, a victim of Aids), Nelly Ntshalintshali, and Wonderboy Nxumalo, who have exhibited throughout southern Africa and internationally.

Small-town KwaZulu-Natal also has several art museums, including that at the Margate civic centre, which has a close association with painter Walter Battiss, who worked in the area for many years; the Carnegie Art Museum in Newcastle with its fine collection of Zulu beadwork and ceramics and of contemporary South African landscape art, and the Empangeni Art and Cultural Museum.

STAGE AND SCREEN
The official home for performing arts in KwaZulu-Natal is the **Playhouse** complex in Durban, which has five auditoriums, including a 1 200-seat opera house.

The complex is home to the Playhouse Company, known for its classical productions, and to the Siwela Dance Company, acclaimed for its cross-cultural work.

Martizburg's largest venue is the **Winston Churchill Theatre** (Leinster Road, Scottsville), which seats around 800 people.

Much of what's lively and stimulating, however, is on show on the university scene and in the small independent venues that have opened up in recent years. The **Elizabeth Sneddon Theatre** on the Durban campus of the University of KwaZulu-Natal competes with the Playhouse as the province's premier theatre. Established in 1981 by the now retired Professor Elizabeth Sneddon, this was the first such enterprise in South Africa to serve a university drama department. Together with the university's Centre for Creative Arts, it offers a huge range of independent productions and is host to a number of annual festivals (book through Computicket).

The university's Maritzburg campus has the **Hexagon Theatre**, known for quality presentations. There's also the **Courtyard** at the Durban Institute of Technology (previously Natal Technikon) in Mansfield Road. The theatre of **Hilton College**, a leading private school outside Pietermaritzburg, presents some excellent productions and is the venue for the annual Hilton Arts Festival.

Durban's **Barnyard Theatres** have opened a 400-seat auditorium in the Gateway Centre. The city's other independent non-funded theatre is **Kwasuka** at 53 Stamford Hill Road, established by Professor Pieter Scholz. Increasingly popular, however, are the various supper-theatre venues, among which are the **Catalina** at Wilson's Wharf on the Victoria Embankment; the **Dockyard Theatre** at the Point Waterfront, with its spectacular view across the entrance to the harbour; the **Backstage Theatre** at the Royal Hotel; and the **Rhumbelow Theatre** on Cunningham Avenue. Performances are also held at the **BAT Centre** in the small-craft harbour off Victoria Embankment.

Screen scene
Until recently KwaZulu-Natal had no outlet for alternative film. Today, however, there is a Cinema Nouveau at the Gateway Centre and an independent alternative cinema at Berea Centre. The University of Natal's Centre for Creative Arts hosts an international film festival in September each year, when a diverse selection of about 100 productions, from about 30 countries and from cutting-edge genres, is screened over a two-week period.

MAKING CONTACT

Margate Art Museum
(039) 312 8392;
Carnegie Art Museum
(034) 328 7622;
Empangeni Art and Cultural Museum
(035) 901 1618/00;
Playhouse Complex
(031) 369 9555,
www.playhouse company.com;
Winston Churchill Theatre
(033) 395 1264;
Elizabeth Sneddon Theatre
www.elizabethsneddon.co.za;
Computicket
083 915 8000;
Hexagon
(033) 260 5111;
Courtyard
(031) 204 2532;
Hilton Arts Festival
(033) 383 0100,
www.hilton.kzn.school.za;
Barnyard Theatre
(031) 566 3045,
www.barnyardtheatre.co.za;
Kwasuka
(031) 309 2236;
Catalina
(031) 305 6889;
Dockyard Theatre
(031) 332 1086;
Backstage Theatre
(031) 333 6000;
Rhumbelow Theatre
(031) 205 7602;
BAT Centre
(031) 332 0451;
Cinema Nouveau
082 16789;
Berea Centre Alternative Cinema
(031) 201 6265;
Centre for Creative Arts
(031) 260 2506,
www.und.ac.za/und/carts

kwazulu-natal

MAKING CONTACT

Rainbow Restaurant
(031) 702 9161;
Centre for Jazz
and Popular Music
(031) 260 3385;
Music on the Deck
(BAT Centre)
(031) 332 0451;
Bean Bag Bohemia
(031) 309 6019;
Le Plaza Hotel
(031) 301 2591;
Rivets *(031) 336 8100;*
Upstage Jazz Café
(Playhouse)
(031) 369 9566/9820;
Awesome Africa
www.livingtreasures.co.za;
Joy of Jazz
www.joyofjazz.co.za;
Splashy Fen
www.splashyfen.co.za;
Southern Cross Music
Festivals *(Dave Falconer)*
(033) 266 423, www.
southerncrossmusic.co.za;
Gorgeous Acoustics
(039) 687 0253,
www.thehibiscuscoast.
co.za/main/events

SOUNDS OF MUSIC

It is in KwaZulu-Natal that *isicathamiya*, a compelling combination of gospel and traditional sounds, emerged and fused with Afro-jazz and other forms. *Isicathamiya* is the style of, among others, the renowned Ladysmith Black Mambazo.

KwaZulu-Natal's music emerged largely in the rural parts of the province, in contrast to Gauteng and the Western Cape, where slums served as the cauldrons of creativity. Durban did, however, have **Cato Manor**, the birthplace of late jazz artist Sipho Gumede.

Notable among Durban's jazz venues is the **Rainbow Restaurant** at 23 Stanfield Lane, Pinetown, a nonracial haven during the apartheid years, and a regular Sunday afternoon jazz spot. With political transformation the restaurant lost some of its allure, but the regular concerts (on the last Sunday of each month) feature some of the country's top bands, and conjure up the memories and sounds of a bygone era (phone ahead to confirm). Another popular Durban venue is the University of KwaZulu-Natal's **Centre for Jazz and Popular Music**, which hosts a jazz evening every term-time Wednesday at seven in the evening. The jazz club (Music on the Deck) at the **BAT Centre** is rapidly becoming one of the city's most popular music drawcards; there are few other places in the country that offer such a relaxed and attractive ambience. Other venues include Bean Bag Bohemia on Windermere Road; Le Plaza Hotel in Broad Street; Rivets in the Hilton Hotel, and the Upstage Jazz Café in the Playhouse theatre complex.

EVENTS

The premier festival on the local calendar is **Awesome Africa**, a celebration of African culture that has a music line-up of *kwaito*, roots, rock, reggae, Afro-jazz and the Standard Bank Joy of Jazz festival. It's held in Durban in September each year, and it complements other festivals associated with the Zulu Royal Month. Ingredients of the latter are the reed dance, the Queen Angel festival and Shaka Day. Initially, Awesome Africa was held in the Shongweni Resources Reserve outside Durban but has recently been moved to the central area's Albert Park in order to support inner-city regeneration.

Splashy Fen is held in April on a farm in the foothills of the 'Berg, 18 km from the town of Underberg. Initially modelled on Woodstock, the occasion was launched, in 1990, with folk, light folk rock and Afro music, the latter featuring the styles of *isicathamiya* and *mbaqanga*. It attracted a New Age following and, even today, has an offbeat reputation, despite its shift into mainstream pop and rock. Each year more than 10 000 people camp out on the farm to enjoy an energetic fiesta, with more than 70 individual performances. In 1997 the organisers introduced a second festival – known as Seriously Splashy – that features classical music and is held in September each year, attracting around 1 000 people.

Splashy Fen has inspired other events, among them the Southern Cross music festivals near Mooi River (contact Dave Falconer) and Gorgeous Acoustics, a music celebration held at the end of August each year at the Oribi Gorge Hotel near Port Shepstone.

More mainstream is the *Natal Witness* **Hilton Art** Festival held in September at Hilton College, one of South Africa's premier private schools, which features theatre, music, dance, art, crafts and books. Also forging a name for itself is Durban Boy's High School, whose Old Club presents the **Not the Grahamstown Festival**, a cheeky take on the National Arts Festival. Here, productions are previewed before heading for Grahamstown.

The prime provincial venue for literary and film occasions is the **Elizabeth Sneddon Theatre** (*see page 61*) the Durban campus of the University of KwaZulu-Natal, which presents the annual Durban International Film Festival, Contemporary Dance Experience, Poetry Africa Festival, and International Festival of Writers (book through Computicket). There have also been efforts to establish a South African Women's Art Festival at Durban's Playhouse complex but this, at the time of writing, was still struggling for support.

THE PRINTED WORD

KwaZulu-Natal's best-known literary son is undoubtedly **Alan Paton**, author of the 1948 novel *Cry, The Beloved Country*. Others with associations with the region include **H Rider Haggard**, author of *King Solomon's Mines* (1885), *Alan Quatermain* (1887) and *She* (1887), who came to Natal as a civil servant in 1875. His writings provide a romanticised image of Africa, inspired largely by his experiences in Natal in the years after the Anglo-Zulu War. His house, Hilldrop – 11 Hilldrop Road, Newcastle – is now both a national monument and a popular B&B filled with memorabilia.

The international poet **Roy Campbell**, of 'The Flaming Terrapin' (1924), and 'Adamaster' (1930) fame, was born in Durban, lived with his family in Musgrave Road on the Berea, and was educated at Durban Boys' High School. Although he was to leave Natal, many of Campbell's poems continued to invoke his memories of early 20th-century Natal.

Campbell's friend and collaborator **William Plomer** was born in Polokwane, in Limpopo province, but penned his greatest work, *Turbott Wolfe* (1925), while living as a 21-year-old at Entumeni, a remote mission station and trading post near Eshowe in Zululand. The novel, which dealt with sexual attraction across the colour line, was enormously controversial and provocative in conservative Natal colonial society. Another writer who was to achieve international acclaim, **Laurens van der Post** (born in Philippolis in the Free State), joined Plomer and Campbell in a seaside bungalow at Umdoni Park near Pennington on the KwaZulu-Natal South Coast, where they lived as part of a small community while working together on the controversial literary journal *Voorslag* ('Whiplash'). This literary trio had little affection for Natal's colonial society (Van der Post referred scornfully to Durban as a 'grocer's paradise'). All three were to leave the country and pursue international fame. Umdoni Park, with its 18-hole golf course and 200 ha of coastal forest rich in birdlife, is open to visitors. Accommodation is available on-site.

AND WHAT'S MORE...

For up-to-the-minute art listings in KwaZulu-Natal, especially the urban centres, visit the websites www.chico.mweb.za/mg/, and www.tonight.co.za; see also the **KZN Tourism** website *www.kzn.org.za, which is updated regularly and is a fount of information on the local arts scene and cultural destinations.*

MAKING CONTACT

Natal Witness Hilton Art Festival *(033) 383 0100, www.hilton.kzn.school.za;* **Not the Grahamstown Festival** *(031) 277 1500;* **Elizabeth Sneddon Theatre** *www. elizabethsneddon.co.za;* **Computicket** *083 915 8000;* **Women's Art Festival** *(Playhouse) (031) 369 9555, www. playhousecompany.com;* **Hilldrop** *(034) 315 2098;* **Umdoni Park** *(039) 975 1320*

Zulu and Afrikaner

Among leading local black wriers is **Oswald Mtshali**, art critic, poet, and famous for his *Sounds of a Cowhide Drum* (1971), who was born in Vryheid. **BW Vilakazi**, perhaps the most important of the Zulu poets, was educated at the Mariannhill Catholic mission, as was **Cyril Nyembezi**, who published numerous novels in Zulu and a book of Zulu proverbs (in English). The poet **Herbert Dhlomo** was educated at Adams Mission near Amanzimtoti. His long poem 'Valley of a Thousand Hills' (1941), which celebrated the great beauty of the land and cried out to the ancestral spirits, was one of the great pioneering works of African literature

Interestingly, although Afrikaans is very much a minority language in the province, KwaZulu-Natal also produced one of the country's leading Afrikaans writers. **DJ Opperman** was educated at the University of Natal, before becoming professor of Afrikaans at the University of Stellenbosch. The 'coloured' writer **Bessie Head** was also born in KwaZulu-Natal – in the Pietermaritzburg mental hospital, where her mother was being confined, although Bessie later escaped racist South Africa to settle in Serowe, Botswana.

Local settings

KwaZulu-Natal has continued to produce provocative literature. The fiendish satirist **Tom Sharpe** lived and worked in Pieter-maritzburg in the 1960s before being deported, and at least one of his savage satires, *Riotous Assembly*, was set in the city. More recently, controversial writer **Mark Behr** set his semi-autobiographical novel *Embrace* (2000) in the Natal of the 1970s. **Jonny Steinberg's** investigative novel *Midlands* (2002) is set in the same territory as *Cry, The Beloved Country* and, like Paton's novel, it explores the deep tensions that haunt a seemingly tranquil country landscape.

Among literary gems that have emerged from the province's Indian community is **Aziz Hassim's** *The Lotus People* (2003), which dwells on the history and culture of his society.

AND WHAT'S MORE...

The centuries-old sites established by some of the greatest regents ever to have ruled in southern Africa form part of an extraordinarily rich and intriguing Zulu heritage. Explore the landscape that was home to Shaka, Dingane, Cetshwayo and their contemporaries. A good place to start is at Ondini, now the home base of the **KwaZulu Cultural Museum** *(035) 870 2050/1/2/3.*

Rising star

Trevor Makhoba, one of KwaZulu-Natal's rising stars, died in 2003 at the age of 47. He was born in Cato Manor but, with forced removals, moved to Umlazi township. In 1996 he won the Standard Bank Young Artists Award and went on to exhibit in Rome, London, New York and the Venice Biennale. His work explored the interface between the traditionl and the modern, and also dealt with controversial issues such as sexual violence and HIV/Aids. Towards the end of his life, Trevor Makhoba was a leading figure in the Anti-Aids 'Breaking the Silence' campaign and his paintings were featured on giant billboards. Makhoba was also a jazz musician. He was described as 'one of the most extraordinary and powerful painters to have emerged in recent times'.

PHILIP HARRISON

WILLIM VAN ZYL

JOHN HARRISON

Castle of Good
Hope, 1679,
Cape Town,
Western Cape

First Muslim
school, 1815,
37 Dorp Street,
Bo-Kaap,
Cape Town,
Western Cape

Vergelegen
manor house, Somerset
West, Western Cape

STACEY SACHS

DISTRICT SIX MUSEUM FOUNDATION

Independent
Armchair Theatre,
Observatory,
Cape Town,
Western Cape

Alf Wyllie Dance
Band, 1952,
District Six,
Cape Town,
Western Cape

Helen Martin's
Owl House,
Nieu Bethesda,
Western Cape

OWL HOUSE FOUNDATION

Evita se Perron,
Darling,
Western Cape

*Crowd and Covered
Monument 1*,
charcoal and
coloured pencil
on paper, by
William Kentridge,
1992

Klein Karoo
Nasionale
Kunstefees,
Oudtshoorn,
Western Cape

WILLIM VAN ZYL

BRIAN BOSHOFF

The Pramberg
('Breast Mountain'),
Kouebokkeveld, a
landmark made famous
by the Afrikaans poet
and writer Boerneef

A lone ox-wagon in
Gamkaskloof, the
setting for André
Brink's *Devil's Valley*

Tamfuti,
ceramic sculpture by
Bonnie Ntshalintshali,
Ardmore Studios,
KwaZulu-Natal

WILLIAM HUMPHREYS ART GALLERY

Restored cottages,
Graaff-Reinet,
Eastern Cape

Korsten,
Port Elizabeth,
Eastern Cape,
the setting of
Athol Fugard's
The Blood Knot

Guy Butler and
Etienne van Heerden
at the grave of Olive
Schreiner, Buffelskop,
Eastern Cape

south africa
in colour

Nelson Mandela
Metropolitan
Art Museum,
Eastern Cape

Dancers, National
Festival of the Arts,
Grahamstown,
Eastern Cape

Musician, National
Festival of the Arts,
Grahamstown,
Eastern Cape

Jazz murals,
Grand Gardens Hotel,
Port Elizabeth,
Eastern Cape

Windmills for sale
on the roadside,
Cradock,
Eastern Cape

Memorial Tower
building, University
of KwaZulu-Natal

south africa
in colour

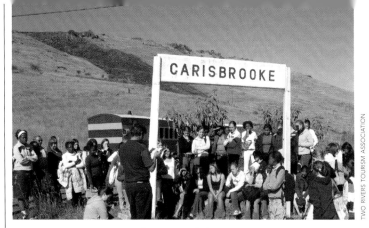

Carisbrooke Siding,
KwaZulu-Natal,
made famous by
Alan Paton's *Cry,
The Beloved Country*

Shakaland
Cultural Village,
KwaZulu-Natal

National Women's
Memorial,
Bloemfontein,
Free State

Detail of gable,
Oliewenhuis Art
Museum,
Bloemfontein,
Free State

Dance of Reconciliation, oil on paper on board, by Frans Claerhout, Oliewenhuis Art Museum, Bloemfontein, Free State

Lourens van der Post Memorial Garden, Philippolis, Free State

Blind Alphabet, wood, by WHA Boshoff, Oliewenhuis Art Museum, Bloemfontein, Free State

south africa
in colour

City Hall,
Johannesburg,
Gauteng

Skyline at night,
Johannesburg,
Gauteng

JOHANNESBURG TOURISM COMPANY

JOHANNESBURG TOURISM COMPANY

Staff at *Drum* magazine, 1955; from left: Henry Nxumalo, Es'kia Mphalele, Casey Motsisi, Can Themba, Jerry Ntsipe, Arthur Maimane, Victor Xashimba, Dan Chocho; squatting: Benson Dyantyi, Ken Mtetwa, Bob Gosani

Market Theatre, Newtown Cultural Precinct, Johannesburg, Gauteng

Carved wooden busts, Mary Fitzgerald Square, Newtown, Johannesburg, Gauteng

MonteCasino, Fourways, Johannesburg, Gauteng

PHILIP HARRISON

SHANGANA CULTURAL VILLAGE

Traditional Ndebele
village, Botshabelo,
near Middelburg,
Mpumalanga

Shangana
Cultural Village,
near Hazyview,
Mpumalanga

Work of artist Nukain
Mabusa on hillside,
Revolver Creek,
near Barberton,
Mpumalanga

PHILIP HARRISON

Oppikoppi music
festival at Northam,
near Thabazimbi,
Limpopo

Musician,
Oppikoppi music
festival at Northam,
near Thabazimbi,
Limpopo

Village Gossip,
oil on canvas,
by Gerard Sekoto,
1946

JOHANNESBURG ART GALLERY

God and Christ,
wood, by
Jackson Hlungwani

Bruintjieshoogte,
near Graaff-Reinet,
enjoys close
associations with
Eve Palmer's
The Plains of Camdeboo

NATIONAL ENGLISH LITERARY MUSEUM

Oom Schalk-lookalike
Egbert van Bart and
smoking companion,
Groot Marico,
North West

Mampoer distillery,
Groot Marico,
North West

Corbelled house,
Gunsfontein,
Northern Cape

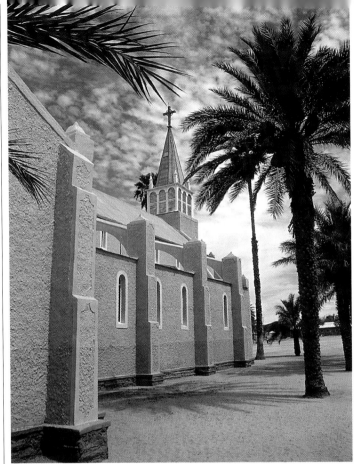

BRIAN BOSHOFF

'Cathedral in the
Desert', Pella,
Northern Cape

San Art Project,
Wildebeestkuil,
Northern Cape

PHILIP HARRISON

ARCHITECTURE

There is very little left of the province's precolonial architecture: the African peoples living along the lush subtropical eastern seaboard used wood and grass in the construction of their beehive-shaped homes, unlike the communities of the largely treeless interior plateau, who used stone. However, in and around the **Valley of the Kings** near Ulundi there are reconstructions of the royal *kraals* of the 19th-century Zulu kings. Umgungundlovu, the site of Dingane's capital, is well maintained and open (daily) to visitors, while KwaNodwengu, where King Mpande established his residence and was buried, is marked with a memorial park and site museum. The most impressive of the royal residences, however, is at Ondini, King Cetshwayo's capital, where the final, disastrous battle of the Anglo-Zulu War was fought (1879). Ondini was burned to the ground by the British invaders but has since been reconstructed and is now the site of the **KwaZulu Cultural Museum**.

Colonial reminders

The province of KwaZulu-Natal offers some excellent examples of 19th and early 20th-century British colonial architecture. It also has many charming religious structures built by missionaries and Hindu and Muslim communities that originated, mainly, in India.

Along central Durban's West Street is the Edwardian City Hall, completed in 1910; the handsome neo-Classical Post Office, and the elaborate facades of once-fashionable department stores such as Greenacres (now Edgars). Along Victoria Embankment stands the old Durban Club, one of the city's most venerable Victorian-era institutions; and on the Berea you'll see some fine Victorian villas. Notable among these are Monaltrie at 59 Musgrave Road, and King's House on Eastbourne Road in Morningside, a fine example of an Edwardian mansion. Also interesting are late 19th-century warehouses and other harbour buildings situated along Point Road, now the focus of a major waterfront development project.

Durban also has some fine buildings from the 1920s and 1930s. The Playhouse was built in mock-Tudor style and renovated in the 1980s.

Perched high above the Berea, at the end of King Edward V Avenue is the Durban campus of the **University of KwaZulu-Natal**.

The Howard College building, with its impressive dome, sliding shutter windows and large central courtyard, is neo-Classical in style with elements of early Art Deco. The Memorial Tower building is yet anther fine example of late Art Deco. Other rather impressive Art Deco structures include Quadrant House at 114 Victoria Embankment; Berea Court located at 399 Berea Road; and Surrey Mansions at 323 Currie Road, Musgrave.

A cry from the heart

Alan Paton's *Cry, The Beloved Country* has a famous opening paragraph: 'There is a lovely road that runs from Ixopo into the hills. These hills are grass-covered and rolling, and they are lovely beyond any singing of it. The road climbs 7 miles into them, to Carisbrooke; and from there, if there is no mist, you look down on one of the fairest valleys of Africa...'

The book is about tragedy and hope, and it is filled with a deep love for the land. The story begins in the wood-and-iron church in the village of Ndontsheni, deep in the Umzimkulu Valley. It was to this church that a small child brings a letter addressed to the Reverend Stephen Khumalo, sent from the mission house in Sophiatown, requesting him to come to Johannesburg where his sister is dangerously ill. In his author's note Paton acknowledges that there is no actual place called Ndontsheni, but he does make it clear that he was thinking of the villages in the Valley when he wrote the story.

Paton gives a magnificent account of the Khumalo's train journey from the valley to Carisbrooke, to Ixopo, and then on to Pietermaritzburg and eventually to Johannesburg. He writes of a 'small toy train' climbing up the narrow-gauge line to Carisbrooke, where there is a magnificent view across the valley.

Much of the remainder of the novel is played out in the city of Johannesburg, where the old priest searches desperately for his son Absalom. In the final section of the book, however, Khumalo returns by train to a desperate and drought-stricken Ndontsheni, where he tells his wife the terrible truth – that their beloved Absalom is condemned to be hanged for the murder of Arthur Jarvis, the son of a white farmer from the very district in which they live. The final, tragic scene is played out on a mountain called Emoyeni above the village of Carisbrooke. Khumalo climbs the mountain to keep vigil at dawn, at the very moment his son is hanged in faraway Johannesburg.

AND WHAT'S MORE...

Capture a sense of what the remarkable Alan Paton was feeling as he wrote his award-winning classic by visiting Ixopo and, in particular, the gracious old **Morning View** *where Alan and Dorrie Paton lived. To see the beautiful home, contact Margie on (039) 834 2941/1337. If there's time, also take a trip to the Carisbrooke railway siding to retrace the forlorn journey of Reverend Khumalo on what is now known as the* **Alan Paton Express**, *(039) 834 2963, 082 374 1417, pea@futurenet.co.za. For further information on Paton's connection with KwaZulu-Natal, call Glynnis Shewan on (039) 835 0284, 083 273 8037 or visit the* **Alan Paton Centre** *(033) 260 5926, www.library.unp.ac.za/paton*

Modern styles

Much like most of the other cities in South Africa, Durban went high-rise in the post-war years, and tall buildings now line Smith and West streets in the central area, along Victoria Embankment, and on the beachfront's Marine Parade and Snell Parade. There is a slight eccentricity to Durban's modernism, as you can see in some of the buildings along the Embankment (most notably number 120, called West Point, and number 136, the IGL building) and here and there an odd hint of Brazilian influence (for example, Las Vegas at 67 Snell Parade), and a touch of Miami Beach in the high-rise hotels of the Marine Parade.

One of the more impressive of the later buildings is 88 Field Street right in the centre of the city, a spiraling, octagonal,

Tracking Paton

Although more than half a century has passed since *Cry, The Beloved Country* was published, Ixopo still attracts a sprinkle of visitors in search of Paton's 'grass-covered and rolling hills'. Within the town itself is **Morning View**, the rambling old house occupied by Paton and his wife Dorrie in the 1920s, when Paton taught at the local school (contact Margie to arrange a visit). Outside Ixopo, on the R56 towards Umzimkulu, beneath the mountain known as Emoyeni and overlooking the great Umzimkulu Valley, is the tiny Carisbrooke railway siding,

It is now possible to follow part of the lonely journey taken by Reverend Khumalo on the narrow-gauge track. The line had fallen into disuse by the early 1980s, and was soon overgrown and neglected. In 2000, however, it was sold off and then partially restored through the efforts of the Natal Railway Museum and the Ixopo Two Rivers Tourism Association. Railway enthusiast Julian Perreira was granted the concession to operate the 'Alan Paton Express' along the historic line. Initially Perreira ran a single inspection trolley to convey visitors from Ixopo to Carisbrooke, but he has since introduced a number of restored locomotives of different types.

The city of Pietermaritzburg also has strong associations with Alan Paton. He was born, on 11 January 1903, at 9 Greyling Street, and lived at 19 Pine Street and 551 Bulwer Street. He studied (and taught) at Maritzburg College and also at the local campus of the University of Natal, where he was president of the Students' Representative Council. Today the University of KwaZulu-Natal hosts the Alan Paton Centre, which is part museum, part archive. Located at 165 King Edward Avenue, it has a wealth of material relating to the author's life. Later on Paton lived in Kloof (23 Lynton Road) and Botha's Hill (14 Botha's Hill Road) near Durban. He died on 12 April 1988 and was cremated at Durban's Stellawood cemetery. See Peter Alexander's excellent *Alan Paton: a Biography* (Oxford University Press).

steel-and-glass structure that was built in the mid-1980s. Also impressive in scale and design is the International Convention Centre (1997) on Ordinance Street, with its large curved roof. Far more modest in scale, but interesting for their architecture, are the BAT Centre on Victoria Embankment, a renovation of an old Navy building (1995); the NSA Gallery at 166 Bulwer Road, with its minimalist finishes,

and the Wiggins-Umkumbane multipurpose community centre on New Dunbar Road, Cato Manor, which is an elegant blend of modern and ethnic themes. Also interesting is the reworking of the old harbour buildings integral to the waterfront redevelopment scheme at The Point. A brash newcomer is the Suncoast Casino and Entertainment World on Durban's Golden Mile, which is a Post-Modern rehashing of Art Deco.

kwazulu-natal

Places of worship

Among Durban's most impressive Christian mission buildings and churches is **Mariannhill**, a Trappist monastery founded in 1882 and once home to more than 1000 monks. St Joseph's Cathedral (1919) at Mariannhill is a red face-brick building in Romanesque style. Also interesting is the basilica (1887), which was the original church; the gatehouse (1907), with its steeply pitched turrets; and the cloisters (1883).

The many elaborately decorated **Hindu temples** in and around Durban add an exotic touch to the cityscape. The most important clusters of colourful traditional temples, dating back to the late 19th century, are along Umgeni and Somtseu roads and on Bellair Road in Cato Manor (see *South Africa's Top Sites – Spiritual*). A remarkable non-traditional building is Hare Krishna's Shri Shri Radha-Radhanath Temple of Understanding in Chatsworth.

The Juma Masjid on Queen and Grey streets accommodates 4 500 worshipers. There are, however, many remarkable traditional mosques.

Also of architectural and historic importance in and around Durban is Adams Mission, near Amanzimtoti, the Mission Church at Groutville (linked to ANC leader Albert Luthuli), the Inanda Mission and the Gandhi settlement around Phoenix to the north of the city, and a large number of traditional and non-traditional Hindu temples and mosques (see the companion volume *South Africa's Top Sites: Spiritual*).

Pietermaritzburg

The provincial capital is known mainly for its red-brick Victorian buildings, the most impressive of which is the City Hall, a remarkable example of a Victorian eclecticism that brings together Classical and Gothic elements in a 'free style'. The original building burnt down in 1896 but was reconstructed in 1901. Among the many other red-brick colonial edifices are the Old Supreme Court on Commercial Road (now the Tatham Art Gallery); the Legislative Assembly buildings at 245 Longmarket Street, with a statue of Queen Victoria at the entrance; the old railway station at the top of Church Street, which has a strong association with Gandhi; the Jubilee Pavilion in Alexandra Park, and the 'Collegiate Gothic' buildings of Maritzburg College in College Road.

More austere are the grey sandstone structures, in neo-Classical and imperial Baroque style, such as the green-domed Legislative Council in Longmarket Street; the Colonial building in Church Street, and the Post Office in Longmarket.

While the best architecture in KwaZulu-Natal is the Victorian and Edwardian treasures in Durban and Pietermaritzburg, there are also lovely buildings elsewhere. These include the Sufi mosque in Ladysmith, the colourful Hindu temples in coastal towns such as Dukuza, the colonial architecture in places like Greytown, and the old republican architecture in Vryheid and Utrecht.

Of word and pen

isiZulu has a rich oral tradition but increasingly, also, a significant written literature. The first Zulu grammar book was published in 1859 and the Bible was translated into Zulu in 1883. The first Zulu novel is believed to be John Dube's *Insila ka Shaka*, published in 1930. After Dube came BW Vilakazi with *Noma Nini* (1935) and RRR Dhlomo's series on Zulu kings – *uDingane*, *uShaka* and *uMpande* – published between 1936 and 1938. In the 1950s the major literary figure was Sibusiso Nyembezi and in the 1960s was OEHM Nxumalo (author of *Ikusasa Alaziwa*). The first major woman writer in Zulu was Joyce Gwayi who wrote in the 1970s and who followed in the tradition of historical romance. In the 1980s CT Msimang dominated Zulu literature and more recently the visionary Zulu poet Mazisi Kunene has achieved considerable acclaim.

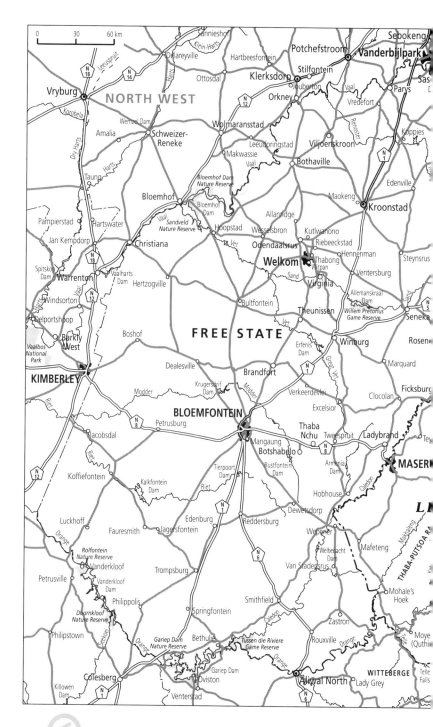

FREE STATE

To many residents of the big cities – Johannesburg, Durban, Cape Town – the Free State may be perceived as somewhat of a cultural desert. The impression is misplaced. The Free State has one of the finest art museums in South Africa, one especially impressive theatre complex, and a number of esoteric and lively music festivals. The small town of Clarens in the Eastern Highlands has emerged as one of South Africa's premier art destinations, while many other of the highveld *dorpe* have associations with some of the country's key literary figures.

free state

AFRICAN HERITAGE

The dominant African culture in the Free State is South Sotho, a group that settled in the region around AD1400. Much later, at the time of the great 19th-century upheaval known as the *difaqane*, its component parts were consolidated into the Sotho nation by King Moshoeshoe. Not long afterwards, the South Sotho came into conflict with the Boers who had moved up from the Cape. The Sotho lost large tracts of their land and many of them retreated into the mountain stronghold of Lesotho (which became a British protectorate). However, many others remained in what is now known as the Free State.

The traditional garb of the South Sotho, who live in a cold part of the country, is the colourful blanket and peaked plaited hat; the premier cultural centre is the Basotho 'living museum' in the Qwa Qwa Nature Reserve (which is being incorporated into the Golden Gate Highlands National Park) about 50 km east of Harrismith on the R12 towards Clarens. Set in the beautiful upland surrounds, the village provides a fascinating insight into the lifestyles and customs of a remarkable mountain people. On site is a museum, art gallery, restaurant, and traditional healers and story-tellers. A special feature is the Matlakeng herbal plant trail – your guide en route is a knowledge *ngaka*, or healer, who is able to explain all about traditional treatments for a vast array of physical and psychological ailments. Basotho pony trips can also be arranged at the village.

THE VISUAL ARTS

Oliewenhuis, on Bloemfontein's Grant's Hill, is a handsome setting for a top-notch art museum. The neo-Cape Dutch mansion, graced by lovely gardens, was home to the premiers the old Orange Free State and, later, to governors-general and presidents of South Africa. It was set aside as a show-case (a satellite of the National Museum in Bloemfontein) and offers an impressive collection of traditional and contemporary art, including works by such figures as Thomas Baines, JH Pierneef, Jan Ernst Volschenk, Gregoire Bonzaaier and Walter Battiss.

Especially evocative among the small but growing contemporary display are Julia Teale's *Silent, Each Contemplating the Other in Mirror of Reciprocal Flesh*, Willem Boshoff's *Blind Alphabet*, a number of works by the Free State's leading artist, Father Frans Claerhout, and the colourful African carousel, set in the lovely gardens, which combines elements of both African and European mythology.

One of Oliewenhuis's features is the underground reservoir discovered beneath the house in 1994, a space that now serves as an unusual setting for exhibitions and special events.

The **Johannes Stegmann Art Gallery**, in the SASOL Library buildings of the University of the Free State's library, is also worth visiting for artworks important to academic study. Represented in the collection are Claerhout, and Penny Siopis, whose life-size female nude, *Terra Incognita* (1991), constructed from oil and photographic collage on board, is especially noteworthy.

Artist retreats

Arguably the two most important places for the visual arts outside the city of Bloemfontein (apart, that is, from the sites of prehistoric rock-paintings and engravings; see other volumes in this series) is **Tweespruit**, where the Catholic priest, Father Frans Claerhout, resided, and **Clarens**, where a large cluster of artists now live and work in an enchanting environment.

The acclaimed Father Claerhout was born in Belgium in 1919 and came to the Free State as a Catholic missionary in 1948. Although he had no formal art training he began drawing the peoples and landscapes of his new home, holding his first solo exhibition in 1961. His art is striking for its colours and the atmosphere it evokes. He spent many years elsewhere, in Krugersdorp near Johannesburg, but then retired to the mission station at Tweespruit where many of his finest artworks were produced. His mission studio may be visited.

The town of Clarens has an extraordinarily beautiful setting in the province's eastern uplands. Named after the Swiss town where the old republican president Paul Kruger died, it has been reinvented as an artists' retreat and a tourist mecca. The catalyst for the emergence of the village as an artists' refuge was the eccentric Martin Wessels, the 'wild man of Clarens', who moved into the area in the early 1980s (unhappily, though, this colourful character left after a dispute with the municipality over the payment of rates).

No fewer than 11 of the 20 Free State artists featured in the *Zebra Register of South African Artists* (2001) are located in Clarens, most of them landscape painters inspired by the beauty and quality of light in the highlands. Especially notable are the landscape oils of Johan Smith; and Simon Addy's and Lyn Hoyles' acrylic-on-canvas works. There are, however, at least 18 art galleries in the town, and, for visitors, numerous tea gardens, coffee shops, pubs and bed-and-breakfast establishments. Painting holidays at Clarens are offered by the Enslin Vorster Studio Gallery, with tuition in both oils and watercolours, and by Marion Townsend at the Sunnyside Guest Farm.

SOUNDS OF MUSIC

Jazz venues are generally quite scarce in the Free State, even in the city of Bloemfontein and the larger towns of the region. Those that have been established here do, however, have a good reputation for some fine jazz. Options include **Moods and Flavours** at 60 Parish Avenue, Bloemfontein, possibly one of South Africa's best jazz clubs and **Corner House Jazz Club** at the junction of Nkoane and Phakati streets in Thabong township situated outside Welkom.

The **Macufe Jazz Festival**, which is sponsored by Standard Bank Joy of Jazz, is held annually at Loch Logan in Bloemfontein. **Tikwe Lodge** in Virginia hosts the Tikoloshe Jazz Festival once a year.

MAKING CONTACT

FINE ART
Tweespruit
Mission Station
(051) 63 0044;
Johan Smith
(058) 256 1620,
www.johansmith.co.za;
Simon Addy
and Lyn Hoyle
(058) 256 1875,
www.addyhoyle.co.za;
Enslin Vorster
Studio Gallery
(058) 256 1312, enslin-vorster@efs.co.za;
Sunnyside Guest Farm
(Marion Townsend)
(058) 256 1099,
townsend@lbrand.com

MUSIC
Moods and Flavours
(051) 432 2864;
Macufe Jazz Festival
(051) 405 4680, 447 7771,
www.joyofjazz.co.za;
Tikoloshe Jazz Festival
(Tikwe Lodge)
(057) 212 3306

free state

EVENTS

The Free State's major occasion is the **Mangaung African Cultural Festival** (Macufe), which draws more than 16 000 art and jazz lovers to Bloemfontein in October each year. The focuses are on youth, heritage and gospel; featured are drama, dance, music, fine arts, and crafts.

Very different kinds of celebration take place at **Rustler's Valley** in the eastern highlands, where New Age spirituality and hippiedom are given expression at Easter, over New Year, and during the winter and summer solstice. The annual calendar for Rustler's includes music, of course, plus African 'sweat hut' ceremonies, earth rites, drumming workshops, 'rainbow horse' dances, 'saucery cooking' holidays, permaculture design courses, and the spring equinox rituals. Hardly the fare one would expect from the Free State! (See also the companion volume *South Africa's Top Sites – Spiritual*.)

PERFORMING ARTS

Free State's premier theatre is Bloemfontein's 1 000-seat **Sand du Plessis** (the building also houses the 260-seat André Huguenot Auditorium), a modern, technically advanced structure that glitters with glass and marble. There's also the Bloemfontein **Civic Theatre** in Markgraaf Street, and the Odeion on Campus and Wynand Mouton theatres at the **University of the Free State**. The most charming of Bloemfontein's theatres, however, is the intimate **Sterrewag**, housed in the old Observatory on Naval Hill.

Welkom has the **Ernest Oppenheimer Theatre** at the civic centre in Stateway Street, widely regarded as one of the best outside South Africa's major centres. There's also the **Ettienne Rousseau** in Jan Vorster Drive, Sasolburg and the **Civic Theatre** in Steyn Street, Kroonstad.

THE PRINTED WORD

Bloemfontein has a distant but perhaps significant association with one of the 20th century's major literary figures: **JR Tolkien** was born on 3 January 1893 on the second floor of the African Bank building on the corner of Maitland and West Burger streets in the central city, now the site of the Price 'n Pride furniture store.

Most residents of Bloemfontein were blissfully ignorant of Tolkien and his links to their city (although there was and is a guesthouse called The Hobbit) until the much-publicised release of the block-buster film *Lord of the Rings* at the end of 2001. The association was quickly and enthusiastically appropriated, and a 'Tolkien Trail' laid out in the hope the city would become a place of pilgrimage for Middle Earth devotees. The major problem, however, is that there's not much to see in Bloemfontein that reminds one of the author.

Tolkien left Bloemfontein in 1895 as a two-year-old child, never to return. Apart from his birthplace, which is now a furniture store, there is the Anglican cathedral in St George's Street, where he was baptised, and his father's grave in the President Brand Cemetery. For more information, contact Jake Uys, chairman of the Bloemfontein Tolkien Society and owner of The Hobbit Guesthouse.

The other literary birthplace is Philippolis. It was here that **Laurens van der Post**, author, philosopher, explorer, and mentor to Prince Charles, started life on 13 December 1906, the thirteenth of 15 children. In 1998, two years after his death at the age of 90, a memorial garden was opened in the centre of the town. Designed by Alida Stewart, it represents a journey from cradle to the grave, symbolising both the physical and spiritual dimensions of life. In the middle of a gateway is an urn containing the remains of Sir Laurens; adjoining the memorial garden is a writers' retreat, the Van der Post Gastehuis.

The Van der Post house in Philippolis has been designated a national monument. Formerly an attractive guesthouse, it is presently being developed as a scientific and environmental centre called the Karoo Institute (for information, contact Doreen Atkinson). In the popular imagination, Van der Post remains an extraordinary and whimsical character, although his reputation has been some-what tarnished by the publication of JDF Jones's book, *Storyteller: The Many Lives of Van der Post*, which casts Van der Post as a 'compulsive fantasist' (a polite phrase for liar).

Black novelists

The Free State also has links with South Africa's first black novelist, **Sol Plaatje**, whose *Native Life in South Africa* dealt with the effect of the Native Land Act (1913) on mainly Free State communities. The contemporary writer **Zakes** **Mda** has set his recent novel, *The Madonna of Excelsior*, in the small eastern Free State town of Excelsior. Based on a true story, it tells the tale of interracial sex at the height of apartheid in a deeply conservative corner of the country. Each chapter begins with the description of a painting by Father Frans Claerhout, whose 'lusty naked black madonnas' (as described in *The Star*) have scandalised the faithful.

Afrikaans writers in a new world

A fine introduction to Afrikaans literature is Bloemfontein **Afrikaans Letterkunde Museum**, in the Third Raadsaal, or parliament building, on the corner of President Brand and Elizabeth streets. Here you'll find rooms dedicated to such notables as NP van Wyk Louw, DJ Opperman, Etienne van Heerden, André Brink and Uys Krige. The museum has made a courageous attempt to come to terms with the changed world, and is by no means the staid and conservative institution one might imagine.

The Free State has special associations with **André Brink**, who was born in the little town of Vrede; **Antjie Krog**, who grew up in Kroonstad, and with **Etienne LeRoux**, who is buried on his farm, Ja-Nee, just outside Koffiefontein. One of the more interesting recent works set in the Free State is Antjie Krog's *A Change of Tongue*, in which she explores social transformations in her home town. In her work, Kroonstad becomes the lens through which one can perceive change in South Africa.

MAKING CONTACT

Van der Post
Gastehuis
(051) 522 2569;
Karoo Institute
(Doreen Atkinson)
(051) 773 0324/09;
Bloemfontein
Afrikaans Letterkunde
(Literature) Museum
(051) 405 4711

ARCHITECTURE

The ruins of the circular **Iron Age** settlements of the Southern Tswana and Sotho peoples are scattered across the Free State highveld. The majority of these ancient ruins are, however, on property that is privately owned and thus not easily accessible, but those visitors who are intent on experiencing the centuries-old civilisations can see reconstructed stone walls and corbelled (or domed) stone huts within the Willem Pretorius Game Reserve.

While there are plenty of examples of both **colonial** and **republican** architecture in the Free State, these are largely unremarkable. There are, however, a few significant exceptions. The small towns of the highveld are generally dominated by imposing sandstone Dutch Reformed churches, and in some places parts of the wider, and charming, 19th-century townscape survives. The settlement of Philippolis, for example, still has streets lined with the simple flat-roofed Karoo homes and the gabled Cape Dutch/Victorian houses of the later period.

The provincial capital

Bloemfontein was originally established as a colonial outpost in 1846 by Major Henry Warden, and not too long afterwards became the capital of a Boer republic that survived until the Anglo-Boer War (1899–1902). The republican state buildings, which still stand proud in the central city (most notably along President Brand Street)

are surprisingly imposing for a country that was so modest in size and influence. They were architecturally influenced by 19th-century French and German Baroque, though these buildings also incorporate some elements of both neo-Classical and Renaissance styles.

The most impressive of all these structures is the **Fourth Raadsaal**, situated off Aliwal Street and now the seat of the provincial legislature. Of the post-republican buildings the most striking are the neo-Classical **Supreme Court of Appeal** (1929) across the way from the Fourth Raadsaal, and the City Hall (1934) at the far north of President Brand Street. Also notable are the neo-Cape Dutch **Oliewenhuis**, which was once home to the prime ministers of the Free State and now serves as an art gallery (*see page 72*) and the **National Women's Monument**, a tall obelisk surrounded by sculptures and a diorama, which serves as a memorial to the 26 000 Boer women and children who died in British concentration camps.

Sasolburg, in the far north of the province, is interesting in that it is a relatively new town: planned from scratch, it was created in the 1950s to house workers in the giant oil-from-coal plant. Designed by Max Kirchoffer, it's based on the British 'New Town' model, but with one difference – there was very strict racial separation, with the black areas of the town unsurprisingly located downwind of the chemical complex.

(*see page 72*)

MAKING CONTACT

Willem Pretorius
Game Reserve
(057) 651 4168;
Fourth Raadsaal
(by appointment only)
(051) 447 8899;
Supreme Court
of Appeal
(by appointment only)
(051) 447 8837;
Oliewenhuis
(051) 447 9609;
Women's Monument
(051) 447 3447;
Bloemfontein
Tourism Information
(051) 405 8489

Bloemfontein and Middle Earth

Bloemfontein-born JRR Tolkien, author of *The Hobbit* (1937) and the epic *Lord of the Rings* (1955), is one of the world's most celebrated literary figures. Tolkien's father died in 1896, when he was four years old, prompting the family to return to England. A few years later his mother died, leaving him orphaned and in the care of the local priest. Tolkien experienced great trauma in the World War I trenches, and his health suffered badly. In 1925, however, he was appointed Professor of Anglo-Saxon Literature at Oxford. His social life has been decribed as 'un-remarkable', but he did have a remarkable talent as a story-teller and his first book, which began with the memorable line 'in a hole in the ground there lived a hobbit', was a considerable success. His second major work, *Lord of the Rings*, took 16 years to complete, but was an immense success, rapidly achieving cult status as the most magnificent example of fantasy literature ever. Tolkien also enjoyed a distinguished academic career, writing nearly 40 books. He died in 1973 and is buried with his wife, Edith, at the Wolvercote Cemetery in Oxford. Recently, the extraordinary interest in Tolkien's work was rekindled with Peter Jackson's trilogy of movies: *The Fellowship of the Ring*, *The Two Towers* and *The Return of the King*.

AND WHAT'S MORE...

African politician, journalist and author, **Sol T Plaatje** was born on the farm Doornfontein near Boshof in the Free State, although his family later moved to Pniel, near Kimberley. His novel Mhudi was the first novel in English to be written by a black South African. He is also famous for his Boer War Diary and Native Life in South Africa, as well as for his translations of Shakespeare into Setswana. Visit the **Plaatje Museum** at 32 Angel Street, Kimberley.

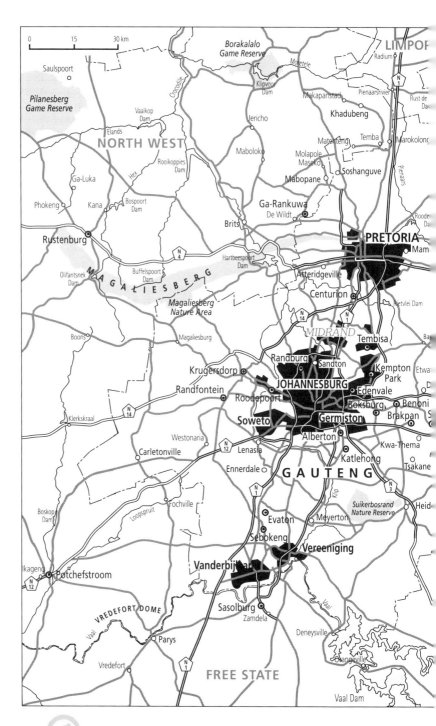

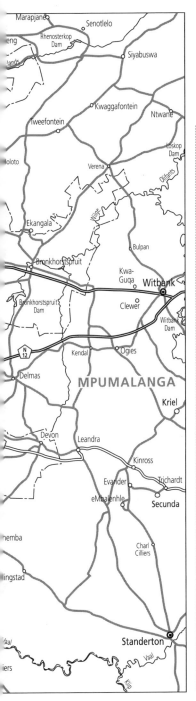

GAUTENG

Johannesburg, also affectionately known as Jo'burg or Jozi, is the country's art and literary capital. Brash and bold, it isn't a place you immediately connect with the arts. And yet this is a city of enormous creativity, the source of its dynamism to be found in its social and political tensions, and in its great human diversity. Neighbouring Pretoria was, historically, a far more stolid and orderly place, and until recently it lacked the 'subversive spaces' that stimulate creative work, but since the demise of apartheid a new liveliness has surfaced, and there is now a vibrant arts scene in a city once dominated by an austere Afrikaner Calvinism.

AFRICAN HERITAGE

One of the more unusual introductions to African tradition in South Africa is the **Khayalendaba** traditional village, immediately below the Oppenheimer tower in Jabavu, Soweto. The village was built, by the African mystic Credo Mutwa, to provide an insight into the spiritual world of his people, and it features bizarre, sometimes grotesque, representations of African deities and spirits. Khayalendaba is included in many of the advertised tours of Soweto; information on touring options is available from Gauteng Tourism.

A recent development is the Ndebele-style cultural village at **Zebra Country Lodge**, which is located in a 400-ha private game reserve about 30 minutes' drive from Pretoria. This is one of the 'Village People' cultural villages developed by the company known as Legend.

The **Sizanani** cultural village in Bronkhorstspruit, an hour east of Pretoria, is also an Ndebele-style complex; it boasts a conference centre, hotel and restuarant.

THE VISUAL ARTS

Gauteng's best introduction to the world of painting and sculpture in South Africa is the Johannesburg Art Gallery (JAG), located in the gritty depths of the inner city.

The Gallery

JAG began life in 1910 as the Municipal Gallery of Modern Art at the Transvaal University College (later the University of the Witwatersrand). It was moved to its present site at the bottom end of Joubert Park in 1915, and is housed in a building designed in neo-Classical style by the noted British architect, Edwin Lutyens. The Irish art dealer, Sir Hugh Lane, originally put together the museum's collection in 1910, at which time it comprised mainly 19th-century British and European works, a selection prompted largely by Lady Florence Phillips, wife of mining magnate Sir Lionel Phillips. Displays were later expanded to include 17th-century Dutch pieces and some modern paintings and sculptures. Emphasis in recent years, however, has been on accumulation of South African art.

Picasso, Monet and Rodin are represented, but it is the South African works that capture the imagination. All the leading local artists are exhibited, among them Irma Stern, JH Pierneef, Cecil Skotnes, Gerard Sekoto, Ernest Mancoba, Moses Kottler, Walter Battiss, George Pemba, William Kentridge, David Goldblatt (a major photographer), Jackson Hlungwani, Noria Mabasa, Bonnie Ntshalintshali, Penny Siopsis, and many, many others. Look out for Wim Botha's *Commune: Suspension of Disbelief*, a lifesize human sculpture, carved from bibles and suspended from the roof; Jackson Hlungwani's carvings; Marc Edward's *Neither known nor unknown*, a human figure, wrapped in a blanket with a table balanced on its ear; and Gerard Sekoto's startling oil paintings.

The major challenge facing JAG in recent years has been its location in an area perceived to be unsafe. The middle-class residents of Jo'burg are perhaps understandably reluctant to venture into the grime and

Khayalendaba
(Gauteng Tourism)
(011) 327 2000,
www.gauteng.net;
Zebra Country Lodge
(012) 346 2229,
www.legendlodges.co.za;
Sizanani
(013) 935 1509,
www.sizanani-org.za;
Johannesburg Art
Gallery *(JAG)*
(011) 725 3130/80/81

apparent chaos of the central city. A few years ago there were indeed some real security problems, which included vandalism and the theft of valuable pieces of art. The relevance of the gallery to its surrounding communities was also questioned, one art critic referring to it as 'an awkward and unwanted Edwardian slab in the centre of the sweaty Joubert Park hubbub'. There was considerable pressure on the gallery to relocate, but JAG director Rochelle Keene remained committed to the central city and responded to the problems with creativity. By 2003 there were strong indications that JAG was back on the map – a new clientele, one that would not normally be associated with art galleries, had been drawn to the gallery as a result of community outreach.

The entrance is off Klein Street in the Joubert Park precinct, an area thronging with minibus taxis and pedestrians. The streets here may seem a bit threatening to a visitor unused to inner-city Jo'burg, but there is safe parking, and the gallery is a secured environment. It is open Tuesdays to Sundays.

Downtown treasures

As appealing and important as JAG is **MuseuMAfricA** in the **Newtown Cultural Precinct** (see page 82), which has a large collection of precolonial and colonial artefacts ranging from rock paintings to such modern sculptures such as Anton van Wouw's *Kruger Reading the Bible* (1907). The museum is not geared to the sophisticated art connoisseur or expert collector but, rather, remains committed to telling the story of South Africa in an accessible and politically

relevant way to a wide audience. Included here is the **Bensusan Museum of Photography**, which holds regular exhibitions of South African and international works.

Nearby, in the **Bus Factory** at the corner of Goch and President streets, are the Artists' Proof studios, which have provided a home for more than 50 mainly young artists. Work is of exceptional quality and has been exhibited internationally. Tragically, in 2003, a fire devastated the studios (then at 1 President Street) and killed Nhlanhla Xaba, assistant director of the enterprise and one of the country's most talented black artists. The event traumatised the art community but, ironically, also sparked a new wave of artistic work dedicated to reconciliation in South Africa. At the entrance to the Bus Factory is an exhibition, in memory of Xaba, which includes surviving relics of his work – burnt fragments of prints that are now part of a large collage (contact Kim Berman). Also in the Bus Factory is the **Shop for Beautiful Things**, which features high-quality crafts.

The **Bag Factory** (known formally as the Fordsburg Artists' Studio), at 10 Minnaar Street on the edge of Newtown, provides affordable studio and exhibition space for local artists who lack their own infrastructure, and creative space for individuals from other parts of Africa and the world. It currently comprises a gallery and 19 studios. The more established artists, such as David Koloane, provide mentoring to younger and new talent; local and international folk mingle to the benefit of both. The Bag Factory is supported by the Triangle Arts Trust.

MAKING CONTACT

MuseuMAfricA
(011) 833 5624;
Bensusan Museum of Photography
(011) 833 5624;
The Bus Factory *and the* **Shop for Beautiful Things**
(011) 492 3696;
The Bag Factory *and* **Triangle Arts Trust**
(011) 834 9181,
www.bagfactory.org.za

The Newtown Cultural Precinct

Downtown Johannesburg, bordered by Pim, Goch, Bezuidenhout, and President streets and focused around Mary Fitzgerald Square (named after an early feminist trade unionist), is South Africa's cultural hotspot.

Newtown developed in the 1970s as a space devoted to resistance politics and to creativity – a place where students, artists, musicians, rastas and revolutionaries congregated in the dilapidated buildings of what was a run-down corner of the city. Today, however, it's the centre of a major urban-regeneration initiative based on the creative arts. Hundreds of millions of rands are being spent restoring old buildings and putting in new infrastructure.

The cultural heart of the precinct is the Market Theatre complex, located in the old Indian Fruit and Citrus Market building near the corner of Bree and Bezuidenhout streets. In 1976, the high noon of apartheid, the theatre courageously began presenting resistance and community drama, and still stages socially relevant and experimental works. Next door is Kippies Jazz Bar, South Africa's premier jazz club, named after the supreme musician Kippie Moeketsi, who died in 1958. Sharing the old Market building is MuseuMAfricA (*see page 81*), which was originally the Africana Museum but has been remodelled as one of South Africa's most innovative and progressive natural and cultural history expositions. Also in the complex are the offices of the French Institute and National Arts Council.

Across Mary Fitzgerald Square, between President and Jeppe streets, is another cluster of activity. Here we have the Workers' Museum, with its startling presentation of life in the old mine hostels; the Artists' Proof Studio (print shops); the Old Electric Workshop (venue for the Johannesburg Arts Alive Festival); the Megamusic centre, with its live performances; the Dance Factory, also known for its performances by national and international artists; Horror Café, with its alternative music events; the funky Shivava Café; headquarters of the urban-regeneration agency Blue IQ; the Beer Museum; the Film Resource Unit; the Drum Café and various clubs, pubs and speciality shops.

Newtown has an impressive calendar of events, which takes in the Johannesburg Arts Alive Festival, FNB Craft Exhibition, Jazzart Dance Theatre, Potters' Exhibition, Women in Jazz Festival, SA Fashion Week, Playtime Film Festival, Provincial Crafts Fair, Barney Simon Young Writers Festival, and concerts by artists such as Gloria Bosman, Moses Khumalo, Ray Phiri, Sibongile Khumalo, Steve Kekana and Norman Chauke.

One of the first phases of the regeneration project was the revamping of Mary Fitzgerald Square, which is now the scene of many open-air cultural activities. Other developments have included: the construction of the Nelson Mandela suspension bridge linking the precinct to Braamfontein, and the new off-ramps from the M1, both of which have greatly improved accessibility. There are plans for an eight-storey-high landmark tower that will provide views across the city; a science centre in the Old Electric Workshop; and an information centre.

City-centre galleries

Inner-city Johannesburg is also home to one of South Africa's best private art collections – the **Standard Bank Gallery** (at the corner of Simmonds and Frederick streets) which, since its inception in 1990, has played a key role in promoting African art. It's seen at its best in the downstairs space; upstairs you'll also find some excellent contemporary South African art and, from time to time, some interesting retrospective exhibitions, among them the work of Gerard Sekota, who died in 1933. Another fine inner-city exhibition space is the **ABSA Gallery** in the ABSA Towers North, 161 Main Street.

One of the country's most innovative and ambitious cultural initiatives is the **Johannesburg Art City Project**, part of the urban-renewal programme. The project has transformed downtown Johannesburg into a large open-air art gallery. At various times – during the lead-up to the 2003 Cricket World Cup, for example – massive artworks have been displayed throughout the inner city, the pieces selected from repertoires of leading local artists and then scanned and enlarged to billboard size. Another form of public art is represented by the 500 or so wooden heads along the streets and pavements extending out from the Newtown Cultural Precinct. This is the work of a small co-operative known as Hand Carving of South Africa, which operates from two small locations near the Electric Workshop in Newtown.

Fashion initiative

Over recent years the city has been promoted as the country's fashion capital through the development of an inner-city fashion project, which takes up 10 blocks bounded by Kerk, End, Market, and Von Weillibh streets. The Johannesburg Development Agency (JDA) supports the initiative and period-ically hosts fashion shows. South African Fashion Week is celebrated in Newtown and at the Sandton Convention Centre in September each year, and features pre-season creations from the country's leading designers, providing a tantalising glimpse into the glamorous world of the fashion industry.

Braamfontein offerings

On the edge of the inner city, is the high-rise office precinct known as **Braamfontein**, once an area in decline but now also the focus of a regeneration programme. One of the anchors of this upgrade is the **Constitution Hill** development, which includes Johannesburg's Old Fort and the notorious prison barracks that held so many of apartheid's political prisoners (see the companion volume *South Africa's Top Sites – Struggle*). Here, in 2004, the new Constitutional Court was inaugurated as a symbol of reconciliation and national unity. A significant feature of the building is its public art, a 200-piece display that includes paintings, ceramics, hand-stitched wall hangings, rock art, sculptures and photographs.

Off Loveday Street is the **Civic Theatre**, which embraces The Premises, a contemporary gallery. The **University of the Witwaters-rand** boasts the **Gertrude Posel Gallery** which, at the time of writing (2004), was being relocated.

MAKING CONTACT

Standard Bank Gallery
(011) 636 6886/4842,
www.sbgallery.co.za;
ABSA Gallery
(011) 350 5139/5793;
Johannesburg Art
City Project
www.jhbartcity.org.za;
Johannesburg
Development Agency
(JDA) www.jda.co.za;
South African
Fashion Week
www.safashionweek.co.za;
Constitution Hill
(011) 274 5300,
www.constitutionhill.co.za;
Johannesburg Civic
Theatre *and* The Premises
(011) 877 6859, www.
onair.co.za/thepremises;
Gertrude Posel Gallery
(University of the
Witwatersrand)
(011) 717 1365,
sunsite.wits.ac.za/
mus/gpg

gauteng

MAKING CONTACT

Goodman Gallery
(011) 788 1113,
www.goodman-gallery.com;
Alliance Francaise
(011) 646 1169;
Art on Paper
(011) 726 2234;
Art Space
(011) 678 1206;
Everard Read
(011) 788 4805,
www.everard.co.za;
Millennium II
(011) 791 5511;
Gallery Momo
(011) 327 3247,
www.gallerymomo.com;
Kim Sacks Gallery
(011) 447 5804;
Manor Gallery
(011) 465 7934,
www.wssa.org.za;
Zuva Gallery
(011) 684 1214,
www.zuvagallery.com;
Mukondeni
(011) 708 2116;
Spaza Art Gallery
(011) 614 9354;
Spark
(011) 485 4602,
orchardsproject@
world-on-line.co.za;
Regina Mundi
(011) 986 2546;
44 Stanley Avenue
www.44stanleyavenue.co.za

Art in the suburbs

The sprawling northern areas of Jo'burg are home to many elegant studios and galleries, the largest cluster of which is found in and around **Rosebank**. Most visible and best known of these northern suburb venues is the **Goodman Gallery** at 163 Jan Smuts Avenue, Parkwood. The Goodman, founded 30-odd years ago, is one of the most important expositions: almost all South Africa's leading contemporary artists exhibit here, among them William Kentridge, whose meteoric career was launched with the support of the gallery.

Other suburban galleries including Alliance Francaise in Parkview; Art on Paper in Melville; Art Space in Fairlands; Everard Read and Millenium II in Rosebank; Gallery Momo in Parktown North; Kim Sacks in Parkwood; Manor Gallery, home to the Watercolour Society of South Africa, in Four-ways; Zuva in Melrose Arch; and the Mukondeni Fine Arts Gallery in Kya Sands, which features the work of vhaVenda artists.

Alternative venues

Most of these galleries are up-market, rather chic venues. In some contrast are **Spaza Art Gallery** at 19 Wilhelmina Street, Troyeville, and **Spark** at 10 Louis Road, Norwood. Spaza provides emerging artists with a route into the mainstream and visitors with innovative local art, unusual craft, a good cup of coffee and a hearty lunch (on Sundays). The owner, Andrew Lindsay, plays a key role in Jo'burg's alternative art scene, producing, among other things, the funky Jozi Maps that present a somewhat different perspective on local theatres, galleries, eating houses, night spots and markets. Spark is housed in a 1930s electrical substation (with characteristic porthole windows) that has been converted into an exhibition and training space for emergent artists. It is supported by the Mineworkers Development Agency, which encourages retrenched miners to develop new sources of livelihood. The gallery is open Wednesday to Friday (contact Pieter).

For a particularly unusual experience of traditional sculpture see **Credo Mutwa's Healing Village**, next to the Ernest Oppenheimer Tower in Dobsonville, Soweto. The bizarre and mystical representations of traditional religious beliefs are now somewhat tattered but still provide a fascinating insight into Mutwa's world. Also striking is the artwork on the cooling towers of the original **Orlando Power Station** (off the Old Potchefstroom Road, the M68).

Soweto in fact is not generally known for its art, but does have one or two other unusual sites, among them the **Regina Mundi** Catholic church at 1149 Khumalo Street, Rockville, widely respected for the role it played during the 1976 Soweto uprising. The church's gallery holds original works by many of South Africa's leading contemporary black artists; the famous *Black Madonna* is to the right of the altar.

A new cluster of alternative art-related activity (galleries, workshops, pubs, restaurants and a bookshop) has emerged in and around the old warehouses at 44 Stanley Avenue, Milpark.

Pretoria's showcases

The **Pretoria Art Museum** is a collection put together in the '30s and after by the city council, and holds works by JH Pierneef, Irma Stern, Anton van Wouw, and Frans Oerder and other white artists, but there is now an attempt to make the collection more inclusive. Most of the city's other venues are devoted to specific individuals.

Until recently, the city supported separate museums dedicated to the work of Pierneef and Coert Steynberg. Many of the artworks, however, have been relocated to the **National Cultural History Museum** at 149 Visagie Street. Pierneef was born here in 1886, and attended the State Model School. His distinctive style, with geometric forms and subdued colours, was influenced by San (Bushman) art and by the European schools of the 1920s, and his paintings, mainly of South African and Namibian landscapes, edged local art away from the realism of traditionalists such as Van Wouw and Steynberg.

The **Edoardo Villa Museum**, located in the old Merensky Library at the University of Pretoria, was designed by the celebrated Gerard Moerdyk. On permanent show are 148 works by the Italian-born Villa; other pieces from the university's art collection are on rotating display. Villa came to South Africa in 1942 as a prisoner of war and remained in the country to become South Africa's premier post-war sculptor. His work was in the European style but responded to its new African context, and his synthesis of different influences was extremely influential in shaping the direction taken by a new generation of South African artists.

The **Anton van Wouw Museum** is housed in sculptor Van Wouw's last home, now also part of the University of Pretoria. The museum displays many of his pieces with other artifacts relating to his work and life. Van Wouw, often regarded as the father of sculpture in South Africa, was born in Holland in 1862 and died in Pretoria in 1945. He was a traditional realist but his sculptures, mainly of human forms, were detailed and conveyed the emotions of his subjects with great subtlety. Some of his work is larger than life, including Kruger's statue in Church Square, but his best creations are his smaller pieces.

The **University of South Africa's** (UNISA) collection is in the Theo van Wyk building on the main campus. It features contemporary South African, Namibian and Zimbabwean art, and has a strong association with Walter Battiss, professor of art in the late 1960s.

For outstanding displays of precolonial art and artifacts visit both the **National Cultural History Museum** at 149 Visagie Street, which boasts one of the country's most innovative presentations, and the **Mapungubwe Collection** in the Old Arts building on the Pretoria University's main campus. The latter is of considerable national importance: it comprises artefacts – including the famous golden rhinoceros and golden sceptre excavated from the capital of the precolonial Mapungubwe kingdom (see the companion volume entitled *South Africa's Top Sites – Science*). The city also has a number of venues that host temporary exhibitions, including the **Association of Arts Pretoria** galleries at 173 Mackie Street, Nieuw Muckleneuk.

MAKING CONTACT

Pretoria Art Museum
(012) 344 1807/8,
www.pretoria.gov/pam;
National Cultural
History Museum
(012) 324 6082;
Edoardo Villa Museum
(012) 420 4017,
www.up.ac.za;
Anton van Wouw
Museum
(012) 460 7422,
www.up.ac.za;
UNISA Collection
(012) 429 6255;
Mapungubwe Collection
(012) 420 3146,
www.up.ac.za;
Association of
Arts Pretoria
(012) 346 3100

gauteng

STAGE AND SCREEN

South Africa's **State Theatre** (now known as the Spoornet State Theatre) is located along Church Street in the centre of Pretoria. Once the heartland of exclusive Afrikanerdom, it is now a vibrant multicultural complex comprising six very different auditoriums ranging from the 1 300-seat Opera House to the 120-seat Intimate and the Arena, a flexible space that can accommodate about 300 patrons.

Like the State Theatre, the **Johannesburg Civic Theatre** complex (off Braamfontein's Loveday Street) has recently undergone transformation. Today, it comprises the Nelson Mandela, Tesson, Thabong, and Pieter Roos theatres, and is widely respected for its local productions and musicals, its spectaculars, comedy shows and pantomime.

Other civic venues in Gauteng include the **Springs** theatre, which has an amphitheatre that can seat an audience of 2 000 and a main auditorium seating 400, and the **Vaal Triangle-Vereeniging Theatre**. The **Pro Musica Theatre**, in Roodepoort, is well known for operatic and classical music shows.

An icon of the liberation struggle theatre in South Africa is the African Bank **Market Theatre** in Newtown, Johannesburg (*see also page 18*). It was established in the mid-1970s as a home for resistance art, attracting many of the country's leading actors and directors, among them Athol Fugard, Zakes Mda, Gibson Kente, Adam Small, Percy Mtwa, Mbongeni Ngema, and Barney Simon, who was to become the theatre's artistic director. Some of South Africa's most outstanding productions were premiered here

MAKING CONTACT

State Theatre
*(012) 315 3165,
www.theatre.co.za;*
Johannesburg
Civic Theatre
*(011) 877 6800,
www.artslink.co.za/civic;*
Springs Civic Theatre
*(011) 360 2290,
www.civictheatre.co.za;*
Vaal Triangle-
Vereeniging Theatre
(016) 450 3024/5);
Pro Musica Theatre
*(011) 674 1357,
http://pmaa.co.za;*
(African Bank)
Market Theatre
*(011) 832 1641,
www.markettheatre.co.za*

Leading light

William Kentridge is widely regarded as South Africa's leading artist; highly respected internationally, his work the subject of solo exhibitions at most of the world's premier centres of contemporary art. Host venues include the Tate Modern in London, the Chicago Art Institute, the Museum of Contemporary Art in Chicago, the Museum of Modern Art in New York, and the Museum of Contemporary Art in Barcelona. He has received numerous awards, among them the prestigious Carnegie Medal, and honorary doctorates from Maryland University, and the University of the Witwatersrand (Wits).

Kentridge was born in Johannesburg in 1955, graduated from Wits 1976 with majors in politics and political studies, and then studied at the Johannesburg Art Foundation (where he also taught) and Ecole Jacques in Paris. He is multi-skilled, having worked in theatre and produced a number of animated short films.

Some of Kentridge's best works are housed in the Johannesburg Art Gallery, and he also has frequent exhibitions at the city's Goodman Gallery in the same city.

including *Woza Albert!* (1981), *Asinimali* (1985), and *Sarafina* (1986). From 1994, the year South Africa saw the first democratic elections, the Market Theatre began to make a difficult transition, losing its fully independent status to become a state-funded playhouse. By 2002 it was under severe financial stress, and there were accusations of financial mismanagement. However, the government stepped in with a cash injection and appointed a new board of directors.

The other once-independent community-oriented theatre that now receives some state funding is the **Windybrow Centre for the Arts** at 161 Pietersen Street (corner Nugget) in the Johannesburg inner suburb of Hillbrow. Sited in a grand Tudor-style mining residence (a national monument), it has three small venues. Its central location tends to discourage middle-class theatre-goers but it does do valuable work in terms of art outreach and community-based productions. The centre also hosts the annual Windybrow Arts Festival.

The University of the Witwatersrand has a number of venues, among them the almost 400-seater Wits Theatre and the small, intimate space known as The Nunnery. The University of Johannesburg, previously Rand Afrikaans University, or RAU, holds theatre productions in the large Sanlam Auditorium. The University of Pretoria's venues include the Masker, Lier and Musaion theatres.

New arenas

Only about one or two truly independent theatres have opened in the province of Gauteng in recent years. In 2000, the renowned impresario Pieter Toerien established the lavish new **MonteCasino Theatre**, in Fourways, after the closure of the historic Alhambra Theatre in the decaying inner-city suburb of Doornfontein. Three years later he opened the smaller Studio Theatre at the same venue. Other theatre venues in Gauteng's new and glitzy casinos are Circus Maximus and Colosseum Showbar at the **Caesar's** casino complex in Kempton Park and The Globe at **Gold Reef City**, the old-style theme-park replica of Johannesburg's mining days.

Another well-known figure who has established a theatre is cabaret artist Richard Loring, who opened **The Sound Stage**, on the Old Pretoria Road, Midrand, in 1998.

Barnyard Theatres have humble Western Cape origins but are rapidly emerging as a leading brand of independents: there are now Barnyard Theatre venues in the Cresta shopping centre, Johannesburg, Broadacres shopping centre in Fourways, Johannesburg, in Alberton, and in the Menlyn Centre, Pretoria. An up-market and increasingly popular venue is **Liberty Theatre on the Square**, on Nelson Mandela Square in Sandton (previously named Sandton Square), a glamorous showplace established in 1997 by producer Daphne Kuhn.

People's Theatre Company
and Off-Broadway
(011) 403 1563,
www.peoplestheatre.co.za;
Showcase Restaurant
(011) 794 4382,
www.theshowcase.co.za;
The Blues Room
(011) 784 5527,
www.bluesroom.co.za;
New Melville Theatre
(Stage Door Theatre)
(011) 482 7981;
Café Riche
Basement Theatre
(012) 328 3173;
Johannesburg
Youth Theatre
(011) 484 1584,
www.jyt.co.za;
Dance Factory
(011) 833 1347;
Cinema Nouveau
082 16789;
Computicket
www.computicket.com;
Film Research Unit
(011) 838 4280/8081;
ZA@Play Theatre Guide
www.chico.mweb.za/
mg/art/theatre;
Tonight
(Independent Newspapers)
www.tonight.co.za;
Gallo Africa
(011) 3409600,
www.gallo.co.za

The **People's Theatre Company** operates as a youth enterprise producing family entertainment. Two main personalities, Gill Girard and Keith Smith, have established a cabaret theatre and supper venue called **Off-Broadway** at 59 Grant Avenue, Norwood, Johannesburg. Other venues for theatre supper are the **Showcase Restaurant** at the Banbury Cross Upper Village, Randburg, and **The Blues Room**, Village Walk, Sandton. Also with a supper-theatre approach is the **New Melville Theatre** (previously the Stage Door Theatre) in Main Road, Melville, which features comedy and cabaret. In Pretoria, there is the **Café Riche Basement Theatre** off Church Square.

Specialist venues in Gauteng include the **Johannesburg Youth Theatre**, at 3 Junction Avenue, Parktown, which specialises in productions for young people, and the **Dance Factory** in Newtown, host to international and local performers and known for its mix of classical and ethnic styles.

The film scene

Guateng's cities have many screen venues, but for alternative or 'art' cinema there are just the Cinema Nouveau theatres in Rosebank Mall, Johannesburg (book via Computicket), and Brooklyn Mall, Pretoria (also via Computicket). These theatres are also venues for special events such as the annual Gay and Lesbian Festival. To buy or view local film and video visit the **Film Resources Unit** on the 3rd floor of 2 President Street.

For production and film listings see the local papers or the ZA@Play Theatre Guide website, and the *Tonight* websites of Independent Newspapers.

SOUNDS OF MUSIC

It was the slums and townships of Gauteng that provided the setting for South Africa's most memorable musical innovations. It was here that styles such as *marabi*, *mbaqanga*, and *kwela* evolved into the vibrant township jazz that so captivates the listener – music created by bands like the African Swingsters, the Manhattan Brothers, and the Jazz Maniacs and such talented individuals as Kippie Moeketsi, Dolly Rathebe, Miriam Makeba, Dollar Brand (now known by his more familiar name, Abdullah Ibrahim), Jonas Gwangwa and Hugh Masekela. It was in the night spots of old **Sophiatown**, venues such as the Odin Cinema, and in Dorkay House, at the end of Braam-fontein's Eloff Street, that it all came together.

Johannesburg's recording studios were the first to bring the exciting new sounds to the notice of the world. The most important of these were the Gallo Africa studios, which today holds the largest archive of South African music.

Probably the biggest musical triumph of the Sophiatown era was *King Kong*, written in 1959 by Todd Matshikiza. It told the tragic tale of South African heavyweight boxing champion Ezekiel 'King Kong' Dhlamini. The show was a phenomenal success in South Africa and, described by one writer as 'the ultimate achievement and final flowering of Sophiatown culture', went on to earn international acclaim, to become one of South Africa's top hits ever.

Superstar from Benoni

One of Hollywood's more celebrated stars hails from Gauteng. Charlize Theron was born in 1975 on a smallholding near Benoni, a gritty mining town on the East Rand. She had a hard upbringing: at the age of 15 her mother shot and killed her alcoholic father (in self-defence, when he arrived home drunk and threatened violence). Despite the adolescent traumas, however, Charlize started on the high road to screen success, studied performing arts in Johannesburg, began a modelling career locally, and eventually threw caution to the winds, heading out for New York and then for Hollywood in search of fame.

Initially, she struggled with occasional acting jobs, but the big break came and between 1997 and 2003 she took lead roles in such films such as *The Devil's Advocate*, *Celebrity*, *The Cider House Rules*, and the remake of *The Italian Job*. Her biggest triumph, though, was her performance as a prostitute and serial killer in the film *Monster*. For this she was presented with a Golden Globe award and the coveted 2004 Oscar award for best actress (the first South African to achieve this distinction). The *boeremeisie* from Benoni had finally made it.

Top places

Among Jo'burg's important jazz venues are Kippies, in Newtown Cultural Precinct (at the time of writing, the club was closed until further notice due to concerns regarding the structure); Back 'o the Moon at Gold Reef City; Blue Moon on Rivonia Boulevard; Julian's Bistro and Theatre in Blackheath; the Radium pub off Louis Botha Avenue in Orange Grove; and the Blues Room in Sandown's Village Walk shopping centre.

Pretoria has the Blue Note Jazz Café on Duncan Street, Hatfield; Café Riche, off Church Square; Kia-Ora Lodge on Jacob Maré Street.

Much of South Africa's most lively jazz is to be heard in the townships, in venues such as are Jazz Fusion Classic Club at 47 Phuphu Street, Mabuya Park, in Vosloorus on the East Rand; Jazz Masters in Soshanguve near Pretoria, and the Referendum Jazz Club in Mamelodi, Pretoria.

Jazz tours and occasions

Organised excursions are now available to these and other venues, which are generally not easily accessible to tourists. Options include the Kwela Tour, Abantu Jazz Tours; Alexandra township jazz offered by Bosele Township Experience; Atteridgeville Jazz, Pretoria; Jo'burg Tours; Cindy's Tours and Imbizo Tours.

Finally, there is the popular **Jazz on the Lake** concert, held in September each year at Zoo Lake just north of central Johannesburg, and the annual **Joy of Jazz** festivals sponsored by Standard Bank. Most prominent of the jazz celebrations are the Johannesburg International Festival in Newtown (August); Jazz in the Park in Vereeniging (September); Jazz in the Park in Mamelodi, Pretoria (December); and Jazz on the Square in Newtown, also in December.

gauteng

MAKING CONTACT

Arts Alive
www.artsalive.co.za;
Voices International
Arts Festival
www.artsexchange.co.za;
Market Theatre
(011) 832 1641,
www.markettheatre.co.za;
Dance Factory (FNB Vita
Dance Umdudo)
(011) 716 3940;
Soweto Arts Festival
082 712 5878;
Alexandra Arts and
Film Festival
072 367 1153,
(011) 463 4971;
Woodstock
www.woodstock.co.za;
Oppikoppi
www.oppikoppi.co.za

EVENTS

Arts Alive, which is held annually in Johannesburg in September, is one of South Africa's largest cultural festivals – more than 500 artists take part – and a great spring awakening for the city. It comprises 10 spectacular days of art, music and theatre, and incorporates the hugely popular Jazz on the Lake concert (see page 89), a joyful occasion that attracts more than 30 000 revellers every year.

The festival is focused on the Newtown Cultural Precinct but, in 2001, it spread its wings to take in events in city's townships and shack settlements, among them Alexandra, Rabie Ridge, Orange Farm, Thokoza and Mofolo Park in Soweto. It also incorporates a number of other, smaller celebrations such as the Festival of Fame, Playtime Festival, and the Women's Art Festival. Arts Alive has a strong African focus, and has come to rival the National Festival of the Arts held in Grahamstown as South Africa's premier cultural occasion.

The other Newtown-centred occasion is the **Urban Voices International Arts Festival**, which is held in July each year and promotes cultural links between Africa and the African diaspora. It features poetry and music, the spoken word, slam, hip-hop, Afro-pop and dub, and black artists from Africa, the USA, Jamaica, France, and elsewhere.

Smaller events are held at the **Market Theatre**, Newtown, throughout the year, among them the Market Theatre Laboratory Festival in May; the Barney Simon Young Writers Festival in October, and the Zwakala Festival in December. The FNB Vita Dance Umbrella, which features performances by local and international artists in February/ March each year, is usually held at the Dance Factory in Newtown, and at the Wits theatre complex.

Although inner-city Johannesburg, and especially the Newtown cultural precinct, remains the most popular venue, local events do take place elsewhere, among them the Soweto Arts Festival and the Alexandra Arts and Film Festival.

Woodstock, which is held at the Heidelburg Aventura Resort in September each year, has a different feel: it features a creative mix of alternative music (including fringe rock) and sporting events such as moto-X, downhill BMX-ing and in-line skating. This is a festival that brings together families (there are many activities for children) with bikers, hippies and New Age devotees.

Oppikoppi, a festival of alternative music (rock, blues and jazz) used to be held over Easter and in August each year at the Fountains holiday resort in Pretoria, but has now moved to a farm near Northam, on the R510 between Rustenburg and Thabazimbi in Limpopo. It is still a highly respected event on the local musical calendar, featuring a great number of talented performers and its absence is sorely missed (see page 110).

THE PRINTED WORD

During its short history Johannesburg has attracted the attention of a host of writers, all either fascinated by its energies or repelled by its aggressive materialism. Its beginnings as a brash mining camp provided compelling material for, among much else, a novel by Francis Brett Young (*The City of Gold*, 1939), and also for the poems of William Plomer (*Conquistadors*) and Albert Brodrick (*Wheel of Fortune*). Writers such as Gertrude Millin (*The South Africans*) and Doris Lessing (*The Road to the Big City*) were attracted by the restless vitality of early 20th-century Johannesburg, but struggled with its reputation for wickedness and its crude tastes and ideals.

Herman Charles Bosman, known mainly for his bushveld tales (*see pages 116–117*), also wrote about the early city, and particularly of the Johannesburg of the 1940s. In his country stories, the city was a menacing presence to which the simple rural folk of Groot Marico would occasionally go in search of fame and fortune, sometimes never to return. However, Bosman had a far more immediate interest in and experience of Johannesburg, and also wrote directly and pas-sionately about the city. His most disturbing book is *Cold Stone Jug* (1949), which recalls his experiences on death row in the Johannesburg Fort (on what is now named Constitution Hill) after he killed his brother-in-law during an argument in 1927 (in the house at the corner of Isipingo and Bezuidenhout streets in Bellevue). Other

writings, including the book *Bosman's Johannesburg* (1986), reflect a nostalgia for the rapidly vanishing (mainly white) early community, but some do suggest an awareness of a city beyond the white suburbs.

Johannesburg's greatest contribution to literature was, however, to come from the experience of those many black South Africans who streamed from rural areas into this great crucible in search of jobs. The 'coloured' writer **Peter Abrahams**, who was brought up in the poor, mixed suburb of Vrededorp, drew from the hardships of these rural migrants in his 1946 novel *Mine Boy*, one of the first major works of fiction by a black South African. However, no piece of writing can really match the enduring power of **Alan Paton's** first novel *Cry, The Beloved Country* (1948), the poignant tale of a rural priest who leaves his home in Natal for the great city in search of his son who, like many others before him, had vanished into the huge anonymity of the place. One of the most evocative descriptions in the book is of the priest arriving at old Park railway station in the central area, a description that captures the awe and confusion that must have been felt by hundreds of thousands of black South Africans when first arriving in the city.

In the 1950s, it was the suburb of **Sophiatown** that prompted South Africa's greatest surge of creative energy. It was here that black writers exploded onto the literary scene, especially in the pages of *Drum* magazine (*see pages 92–93*).

AND WHAT'S MORE...

Herman Charles Bosman *had a long association with Johannesburg. He was educated at Jeppe Boys' High and at Wits University, and died at Edenvale Hospital in 1951 at the age of only 46. He is buried in Westpark Cemetery off Beyers Naudé Drive (grave no. 3942/3 in Section DRM, Block A). It was in Johannesburg that one of the greatest tragedies of his life occurred – at 19 Isipingo Road, Bellevue, he accidentally killed his stepbrother during an argument for which he was sentenced to death. To celebrate the life of this great writer, visit one of his favourite haunts, the charming* **Radium Pub** *(the oldest drinking hole in the city) at 282 Louis Botha Avenue, Orange Grove, (011) 728 3866, www.theradium.co.za. Also read* Bosman's Johannesburg, *edited by Stephen Gray (Human & Rousseau).*

Gems of talent from a slum

Today **Sophiatown** is a memory rather than a place, for there is almost nothing in the streets and homes of the now white (though slightly greying) working-class suburb that reminds one of the racy slum from which poured so much creativity. Happily, however, the memory is preserved in the writings of the *Drum* magazine journalists – Can Themba, Bloke Modisane, Nat Nakasa, Casey Motsisi, Arthur Maimane, Lewis Nkosi, and Todd Matshikiza – as well as in the writings of the 'meddlesome priest', Father Trevor Huddleston, and in the music of Dolly Rathebe, Miriam Makeba, Hugh Masekela, the Jazz Maniacs, and the astounding musical, *King Kong* (*see bottom left*).

The Sophiatown of the 1950s was memorably described by Can Themba in his short story 'Crepuscule':

'It was the best of times, it was the worst of times; it was the age of wisdom, it was the age of foolishness; it was the season of Light, it was the season of Darkness; it was the spring of hope, it was the winter of despair; we had everything before us, we had nothing before us, we were all going directly to heaven, we were all going direct the other way...'

The tensions and contradictions of life in Sophiatown, and of the horror of the forced removals that eventually destroyed the community, were captured in the works of many of the other *Drum* journalists. Bloke Modisane's *Blame Me on History* speaks of Sophiatown as:

'A complex paradox which attracted opposites; the ring of joy, the sound of laughter, was interspersed with the growl and the smell of insult; we sang our sad happy songs, were carried away by our erotic dances, we whistled and shouted, got drunk and killed each other.'

In a disturbing autobiography, Modisane draws a parallel between the destruction of the slum and his own personal disintegration:

'Something in me died, a piece of me died, with the dying of Sophiatown...In the name of slum clearance they had brought the bulldozers and gored into her body, and for a brief moment, looking down Good Street, Sophiatown was like one of its own many victims; a man gored by the knives of Sophiatown, lying in the open gutters, a raisin in the smelling drains, dying of the multiple stab wounds, gaping wells gushing forth blood; the look of shock and bewilderment, of horror and incredulity, on the face of the dying man. My Sophiatown was a blitzed area which had suffered the vandalism of political conquest, a living

The sensational Sophiatown jazz opera, **King Kong***, tells the tragic story of heavyweight boxing champion and township legend Ezekiel Dhlamini. In the story, Ezekiel once enjoyed the prospect of a successful international career, but was sentenced to 12 years' hard labour for killing his girlfriend, and eventually committed suicide by drowning on a prison farm at the age of only 31. The musical premiered at Wits University's Great Hall and went on to success in the USA and London's West End, launching the glittering careers of Tod Matshikiza, Miriam Makeba and Hugh Masekela, among others.*

A small corner of India

The suburbs of **Pageview** and **Fordsburg** (popularly known as 'Fietas') also feature in literature: they were home to Jo'burg's diverse Indian community until the government forced the Indian population to move to Lenasia.

Ahmed Essop's nostalgia for a community life destroyed in the 1970s is evident in his short stories. These include 'Haji Musa and the Hindu Fire-Walker', 'The Yogi', 'Mr Moonreddy', and 'The Betrayal', collected in volumes such as *The Haji and Other Stories* (1978).

memorial to the vengeance of Dr Hendrik Frensch Verwoerd... I could not see the scars and feel the wounds of my life which Sophiatown and South Africa had gored into my body. And there in the dark I could see the Three-Star knives of Sophiatown, their pointed blades zeroed on my body, and I was alone, my body exposed to the naked ugliness of my life, afraid of the things which had montaged the destruction of my soul against that of Sophiatown; I could not tell us apart.'

Sophiatown also featured in the writings of liberal white authors, in particular Alan Paton's *Cry, The Beloved Country* (1948) and Nadine Gordimer's *World of Strangers* (1958), which tells the story of an English publisher, Tony Hood, who moves between the pretentious wealth of the northern suburbs of Johannesburg and the vibrant squalor of Sophiatown and other settlements around the city.

By the time *World of Strangers* was published, the cultural explosion of 1950s had peaked and the dark shadow of removals had crept over Sophiatown. The much-loved priest Trevor Huddleston, who ministered from Christ the King Anglican church, wrote the book *Naught for Your Comfort* in a desperate attempt to preserve the memory of a place that he described as 'positively sparkling with life'. Huddleston feared that the memory of Sophiatown would 'slip away into history'.

Sophiatown was destroyed, but its memory became a powerful icon of resistance and is a continuing inspiration to artists and writers.

After the removals, a white working-class suburb was built on the ruins of Sophiatown and tastelessly named Triomf (meaning 'triumph'). Gone were the places associated with the extraordinary life and energy of place – the Odin Cinema, Chip's Shop, Martha's Shebeen, Fatty's Shebeen, 'Thirty-Nine Steps'. A few of the buildings did survive, among them Christ the King church and the largish house belonging to Dr Alfred Xuma, one-time president of the ANC (73 Toby Road). The street names were also kept: Good Street, Gerty Street, Bertha Street (where Modisane was born), Gold Street, Edward Road, Victoria Road (where the youth of Sophiatown battled the police), Tucker Street and Meyer Street.

Surprisingly, the bland new suburb inspired a prize-winning novel – Marlene van Niekerk's *Triomf*, an account of the dysfunctional lives of the white working class. It was initially written in Afrikaans, but has been translated into English.

Voices from the townships

Soweto was the subject of a number of poems and novels, especially after the youth uprising of 1976 focused world attention on the great sprawling conglomeration of townships. **Oswald Mtshali's** *Sounds of a* *Cowhide Drum* (1971), however, provided evocative images of Soweto prior to '76.

The human agony of state repression after the uprising was also expressed in poems by artists such as Mfika Gwala, and many others who echoed the pain.

gauteng

READ ALL ABOUT IT!

There has been a number of books – both fiction and non-fiction – published on Johannesburg recently.

FICTION
• *Ivan Vladislavic,*
The Restless Supermarket
(David Philip Publishers)
• *Ivan Vladislavic,*
The Exploded View
(Random House)
• *David Cohen, People*
Who Have Stolen From
Me *(Picador Africa)*
• *Pamela Jooste, People*
Like Ourselves *(Doubleday)*
• *Norman Ohler,*
Ponte City
(David Philip Publishers)
• *Joanne Richards,*
Sad at the Edges
(Stephan Phillips)
• *Phaswane Mpe,*
Welcome to Our Hillbrow
(KZN University Press)
• *Heidi Holland and*
Adam Roberts, From
Jo'burg to Jozi *(Penguin)*
• *Adam Roberts and*
Joe Thloloe, Soweto
Inside Out *(Penguin)*

In the post-1976 era there was a spate of angry political novels that dealt with the Soweto troubles. They included **Wally Serote's** *To Every Birth its Blood* (1981), **Sipho Sepamla's** *A Ride in the Whirlwind* (1981), and **Miriam Tlali's** *Amandla* (1981). In 1985 Soweto's leading woman activist, **Ellen Kuzwayo**, told the story of her life and struggle in *Call Me Woman*.

The other township that excited literary interest was Alexandra. The poet Wally Serote had an intense attachment to the place; his poem 'Alexandra' compares the township to his mother – a tough, cruel mother whom he loves desperately.

Serote also wrote of the inner city in 'City Johannesburg', but unlike Alexandra, for which he felt so much affection, the central area was alien, a space where he felt a terrible impotence against the power of white capital.

Perhaps the most awful place in the inner city during the apartheid years was **John Vorster Square**, headquarters of the security police in downtown Johannesburg, a building in which numerous political detainees died under mysterious circumstances. The horror of the Square was best captured by Christopher van Wyk's *In Detention*:

The black literary scene was dealt a severe blow in December 2004 with the death of the author Phaswane Mpe at the age of only 34. Mpe grew up in a small village near Polokwane in Limpopo, and went on to become a lecturer and doctoral student at Wits. His first novel, *Welcome to Our Hillbrow*, dealt with xenophobia and HIV/Aids in this inner-city suburb.

The white writers

While much of the writing under apartheid focused on township life, political resistance and the traumas experienced by the black African communities, there were also accounts of life in the white suburbs. The most notable of the writers is **Nadine Gordimer**, who was born in the gritty mining town of Springs and whose first novel, *The Lying Days* (1953), was set in Atherton, a fictitious mining town that was clearly based on her place of birth. *In the World of Strangers* (1958) Gordimer explored the bourgeois world of Johannesburg's northern suburbs, which she set against the vibrancy and poverty of the black townships of the 1950s. Gordimer's subsequent works continued to take as their theme the nature of personal relationships within the context of political struggle in South Africa, and Johannesburg remained an important setting for her tales.

Other accounts of white South Africa include **Pamela Jooste's** book *Frieda and Min* in working-class Germiston, and **Stephen Gray's** poem 'Mayfair':

The final years of Apartheid were violent and bleak, and a sense of hopelessness seemed to pervade the city – a mood captured in the **David Robbin's** *Wasteland* (1987). Robbins described the whites of Johannesburg as the 'degenerate suburban heirs' of Joseph Conrad's Mr Kurtz – the torch-bearer of civilisation in 'darkest Africa' who succumbed 'to the mad visions born of a craving for total power'. For Robbins, Johannesburg 'had no centre, only a void'.

The modern scene

Post-apartheid Johannesburg is a bewildering, contradictory place. It has an extraordinary energy which, as we've noted, has both fascinated and repulsed writers. The writer **Rian Malan**, for example, views the metropolis as 'one of the ugliest cities on earth', and yet insists that it is a wonderful place to be. Malan contributed a memorable passage to **Heidi Holland** and **Adam Robert's** *From Jo'burg to Jozi* – a book that includes 60 short pieces on an 'infamous city'.

One of the most energetic – as well as feared – places in contemporary Johannesburg is the high-rise suburb of Hillbrow, which has inspired some of the best of the recent work. **Ivan Vladislavic's** *The Restless Supermarket* describes Hillbrow's 'makeover from frayed Euro-café society to shabby Afro-soul' (*Sunday Times*, 21 July 2002), while **Phaswane Mpe's** novel *Welcome to Our Hillbrow* tells the story of a young man from a rural village who confronts love and betrayal in the chaos of Hillbrow. In his encounters with child prostitution, violence, Aids, drug addiction, and suicide, we are provided with a rather disturbing window into South Africa's most complex urban area. Another contemporary account of the life in the city is **Jonathan Morgan's** *Finding Mr Madini*, which tells of the disappearance of a street poet and the desperate search for him in the underbelly world of the city's prisons, hospitals and morgues.

Johannesburg, one of the world's most complex cities, nevertheless continues to inspire an energetic literature that portrays both the malevolence of the city and its extraordinary energy and exhilaration.

It is Johannesburg, rather than Pretoria, which has inspired great literature. However, Pretoria has produced some significant authors – **Christopher Hope, Eugene Marais,** and **Can Themba** are among the writers born in this city. The most significant literary reference to Pretoria is Es'kia Mphahlele's *Down Second Avenue*, a semi-autobiographical account of life in Marabastad, a vibrant, racially mixed, inner-city slum that is reminiscent of Sophiatown.

ARCHITECTURE

Despite its youth, Johannesburg has an interesting and varied architecture. Although much of the early town has been destroyed, there are some interesting remnants of the Victorian and Edwardian eras. Examples include the now almost derelict and sadly neglected Rissik Street Post Office, with its red face-brick *palazzo* façade, opposite the City Hall; the great iron frame of the original Park Station, now standing isolated between Newtown and the railway shunting yards; the Old Fort and gaol on Constitution Hill in Braamfontein, and the grand homes of the 'Randlords' (the early mining magnates) along Parktown Ridge to the north of the inner city (which can be visited as part of tours organised by the Parktown and Westcliff Heritage Trust).

Styles of the past

Edwardian Johannesburg was solid and imposing, reflecting the power and confidence of the early 20th-century mining elite. The grand buildings of this period – bank buildings, mining houses and old department stores – still stand proud in the inner city, along Harrison, Commissioner, Fox, Eloff, President, Main and Simmonds streets.

The most important of these old buildings is the Corner House at the intersection of Commissioner and Simmonds streets. Other notable edifices of the period include the City Hall; the Johannesburg Art Gallery on the edge of Joubert Park (designed by Sir Edward Lutyens); and the Rand Regiments' Memorial, an imposing arch, adjacent to the Johannesburg Zoo at the end of Saxonwold Drive. A very different type of building is the Municipal Market (1913) in Newtown, with its great steel trusses, which now houses MuseuMAfricA and the Market Theatre. In the 1920s the University of the Witwatersrand was built in Braamfontein in imposing neo-Classical style.

The stern elegance of the Edwardian era gave way to the Art Deco of the 1930s, with its vertical fins, flying cornices, flagmasts and plaster relief panels (often with Egyptian themes). One of the first post-Edwardian buildings, influenced by American fashion, was the rather odd-looking 10-storey Barbican building, built in the 1920s, that stands derelict along Rissik Street at right angles to the Post Office.

Many of the buildings dating from the 1930s are now in a rather shabby or even dilapidated state, but still represent an Art Deco treasury. Among some good examples are Astor Mansions at 178 Jeppe Street; Castle Mansions at 89 Eloff Street; Dawson's Hotel at the corner of Van Brandis and President streets; Dorchester Mansions at 73 Rissik Street; the Federal Hotel situated at the corner of Commissioner and Polly streets; Gallo Africa at the corner of President and Troy streets; Stanhope Mansions in Plein Street; and the Union Castle building at the corner of Loveday and Commissioner streets. The monumental headquarters of Anglo American Corporation at 44 Main Street, the heartland of mining capital in South Africa, is also of the period but, unlike the others, is not high-rise.

The East Rand

The crescent of towns to the east of Johannesburg-Pretoria also boasts a remarkable number and variety of Art Deco edifices, many of them magnificently preserved. The city of Springs, with 34 such, is believed to have the second largest collection of small-scale Art Deco buildings in the world (after Miami in Florida, USA), while the main streets of Germiston and Benoni are filled with representatives of the genre, together with some good examples of Art Nouveau. For tours of the architecture – and other aspects – of the region, contact Frans Swart.

AND WHAT'S MORE...

Experience for yourself the grand old architecture of the East Rand – from Art Deco to Victorian. Many of the buildings, particularly those in the older suburbs of these towns, are remarkable and well worth exploring, even on foot. To arrange a guided tour, call Frans Swart on (011) 360 2142/3.

The new styles

By the late 1930s the Modern (or International) movement of Le Corbusier had arrived in South Africa, the impetus coming largely from the energy of the University of the Witwatersrand (Wits) architecture professor, **Rex Martienssen**. The Hillman building at Wits is a fine example of the new idiom; a variant is densely packed Hillbrow (which went high-rise in the 1950s). Hillbrow reflects the influence of a Brazilian version of Modernism associated with Oscar Niemeyer. In the late 1960s and early '70s there was a building boom in downtown Johannesburg, and the skyline soon looked like that of a large American city.

Perhaps the most impressive of the developments was the 200-m, 50-storey-high Carlton Centre, which covered four city blocks and was, at the time of its completion, the highest reinforced concrete building in the world. Inner-city decline has diminished its glamour, but it is still worth a visit for the 50th-floor Skyrama, which provides spectacular views across the city.

While the architecture of the Modern movement was financed mainly with private capital, there were also some notable large-scale public buildings constructed in the '60s and '70s. Among these are the Johannesburg Hospital on Parktown Ridge, which appears as a great slab on the city skyline; the architecturally intimidating Civic Centre on the crest of the hill in Braamfontein, and the large semicircular campus of the Rand Afrikaans University (RAU; now part of the University of Johannesburg) in Auckland Park.

The recent past

The 1980s and '90s brought **Post-Modern** architecture to Jo'burg, much of it criticised as symbolic of a rampant materialism. Examples are the malls and casinos, perhaps the most grandiose of them MonteCasino, a fake Italian hill-top village in Fourways that provoked Mark Gevisser to write of 'the obsenity of a gargantuan casino… its ramparts leering over Johannesburg in a nightmarish reincarnation of the mining town's bawdy past'. Similar complexes are Caesar's near the Johannesburg airport and the Gold Reef City casino.

There are, however, a number of stylish developments from the recent past: Nelson Mandela Square in Sandton, for example, Melrose Arch in Illovo, the African Art Centre in Rosebank, the Apartheid Museum adjacent to garish Gold Reef City, and the Nelson Mandela Bridge between Braamfontein and Newtown. The architecture of Melrose Arch is bold and cheerful. The African Craft Market, on a much smaller scale, is also a joyful development.

The Apartheid Museum, however, is a very different sort of building, an austere prison-like structure that captures the horrors of race segregation. The interior spaces are sombre, dungeon-like – and the whole is a magnificent monument to the human spirit. The Nelson Mandela Bridge, over the railway marshalling yards between the Newtown and Braamfontein, celebrates an icon of the liberation struggle. It is now an important city landmark in the city, rivalling the Hillbrow tower, and the cylindrical Ponté Building, which also stands high on the Hillbrow Ridge.

READ ALL ABOUT IT!

For a detailed account of the architecture of Johannesburg from the 1880s to the 1970s, read Clive Chipkin's Johannesburg Style (David Philip Publishers). See also Hilton Judin and Ivan Vladislavic's BLANK: Architecture, Apartheid and After (Distributed Art Publishers)

South Africa's so-called coloured community has produced a number of very important writers and artists, including Alex La Guma from District Six, Cape Town; Peter Abraham, born in Vrededorp, Johannesburg; and Bessie Head, famously born in Pietermaritzburg's mental hospital. Artists include sculptor and painter Willie Bester, from Montagu in the Western Cape and Bernadette Searle, who uses her art to explore questions of colour and identity in the new South Africa. Also using his own identity to confront racial stereotypes is Cape Town comedian Marc Lottering.

The state capital

Pretoria also boasts an impressive architectural heritage. **Church Square** is the place to begin – it resonates with history, serving as the city's focal point right from its birth in 1855, three decades before the eventually larger city of Johannesburg was founded.

The current form of the square, designed by Vivian S Reeth Poole in 1912, is in fact modelled on Trafalgar Square in London and Paris's Place de la Concorde. In the middle stands the statue of Paul Kruger, who looks sombrely, and perhaps disapprovingly, on the mainly black people relaxing in a park that they were once barred from using. Around the square are some of the handsomest of the country's buildings, the styles varying from neo-Classical, Italian Renaissance and French and German Baroque to Art Deco and Art Nouveau. They include the Old Raadsaal (legislative building), the Palace of Justice (famous as the site of the 1960s Rivonia Treason Trial), the old Reserve Bank building, the General Post Office and the dainty Café Riche building. The square no longer has a place of worship, but along Church Street to the west is the Paul Kruger church, directly adjacent to Paul Kruger's surpisingly humble house (now a museum), where the crusty old president would greet citizens from the veranda.

Three blocks to the east of Church Square, down through a busy pedestrian market, is **Strijdom Square**. Until fairly

recently the place hosted a great bronze bust of the apartheid-era prime minister, JG Strijdom, but the bust collapsed dramatically when the roof of an underground parking garage caved in – on Republic Day, 31 May 2001.

Across the way from Strijdom Square is the Victorian-style Sammy Marks building, which is named after a prominent Jewish philanthropist and industrialist who had a close relationship with Paul Kruger, and who has left a large legacy to the city. The rambling Sammy Marks House (open to the public) is to the west of Pretoria, along the R104 – a relaxing place to spend a Saturday or Sunday afternoon.

Inner-city Pretoria also has some impressive high-rise modern buildings. Look out for the Reserve Bank building, the State Theatre and Opera House off Strijdom Square, and the tall, somewhat unusual Sanlam building located just above Strijdom Square.

There are a number of impressive structures in and around the late-Victorian style **Burgers Park** (at the corner of Andries and Jacob Maré streets). These include a Victorian bandstand and Art Nouveau curator's house in the park; the neo-Medieval Barton Keep with its eerie-looking portals and turrets; Melrose House (1886) opposite the park and open to the public as a museum and art gallery, and the Railway building (at the intersection of Scheiding and Railway streets), designed by Sir Herbert Baker and recently restored after commuters, angry at long delays, set fire to it.

Baker's best

Among the country's more beautiful structures are the **Union Buildings** on Meintjeskop, overlooking the central city. They, too, were designed by Sir Herbert Baker (who was brought to the Transvaal by Lord Alfred Milner after the Anglo-Boer War) and completed in 1913. Although neo-Classical in design, Baker took care to ensure that they blended with the African landscape. Their focus is a great amphitheatre fringed by the semicircular, colonnaded main edifice. The two symmetrical wings of the building extend directly outwards from the amphitheatre; below are well-tended gardens that are graced by statuary.

Although the Union Buildings represented an English colonial heritage they were appropriated by both the Afrikaner nationalist and post-apartheid governments. The amphitheatre, for example, was the place where Nelson Mandela was inaugurated as the first president of a democratic South Africa, and the buildings now house the office of the State President and the ministry of Foreign Affairs.

Memorial and campus

The **Voortrekker Monument**, set on a hilltop to the south of the city (off Eeufees Drive), is the shrine to an Afrikaner nationalism that now belongs to the past. It was designed by Gerard Moerdyk, who was influenced by the *Volkerschlacht* memorial in Leipzig Germany, but also drew inspiration from the Voortrekker icon, the circular *laager*, and, ironically, from the patterns and motifs of the ruins of Great Zimbabwe across the Limpopo to the north. Construction began at the time of the Great Trek centenary celebrations in 1938, and ended a decade later.

The **University of Pretoria**, founded in 1911, has a lovely campus graced by a number of historic buildings. At the entrance on Lynnwood Road, to the east of city centre, is the replica of Kya Rosa, the home of the Jewish businessman Leo Weinthal, who founded the *Pretoria News* and was a staunch late 19th-century supporter of Paul Kruger before shifting his allegiance to Cecil John Rhodes. It's an odd-looking structure with quirky decorations. More imposing is the Ou Letteregebou (Old Arts building) in the historic heart of the campus, built with sandstone in French Renaissance style. Also of importance is the Old Merensky Library, also designed by Gerard Moerdyk. The library, built with granite, has a monument-like appearance and is designed in a Persian-like style, drawing on emblems (such as the zigzag chevron patterns) from the Great Zimbabwe ruins. The **University of South Africa (UNISA)** is very different in form. It is a massive, aeroplane-shaped modern structure, immediately to the south of the city, that fits somewhere in the transition period from Modern to **post-Modern**.

For glitzy post-Modern architecture, visit the huge Menlyn Park shopping centre in the eastern suburbs (corner of Atterbury Road and Lois Avenue in Menlyn).

MAKING CONTACT

Melrose House
*(012) 322 2805,
www.melrosehouse.co.za;*
Café Riche
(012) 328 3173;
Voortrekker Monument
(012) 326 6770;
Union Buildings
(012) 300 5200;
University of Pretoria
*(012) 420 4111,
www.up.ac.za;*
University of South
Africa *(Unisa)*
*(012) 429 4111,
www.unisa.ac.za*

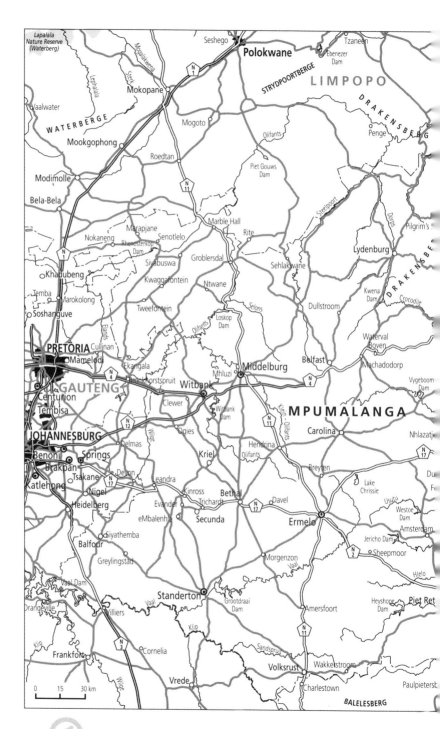

MPUMALANGA

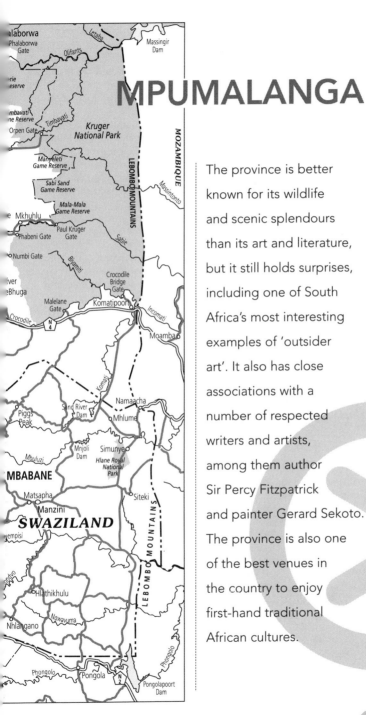

The province is better known for its wildlife and scenic splendours than its art and literature, but it still holds surprises, including one of South Africa's most interesting examples of 'outsider art'. It also has close associations with a number of respected writers and artists, among them author Sir Percy Fitzpatrick and painter Gerard Sekoto. The province is also one of the best venues in the country to enjoy first-hand traditional African cultures.

AFRICAN HERITAGE

Mpumalanga is home to the Ndebele, Shangaan, Zulu, Swazi and Tsonga. When the Boers trekkers arrived in the area in the mid-19th-century, the Pedi (related to the Sotho) were the dominant power, and for many decades the Pedi kings of Sekhukhuneland kept them (and, later, the British) at bay, inflicting a particularly severe defeat on the Boers in 1876. The Ndebele and Swazi, broadly related to the Zulu, were part of the Nguni-triggered migrations of the 18th and 19th centuries. The Shangaan are more directly related to the Zulu: the founder of the Shangaan nation, Soshangana, was sent by King Shaka to conquer the Tsonga people in a region that is now part of Mozambique. The story, however, is that Soshangana was so pleased with the fertile lands he passed through he decided not to return to Zululand. The Tsonga people still live mainly in Mozambique but there is an over-spill into South Africa. They have become closely linked with the Shangaan but there are distinctive practices (such as a focus on fishing rather than the keeping of cattle).

Living museums

The **Shangana Cultural Village** is one of the largest of its kind in the country, competing in size with Lesedi in North West (*see page 112*) and Shakaland and Dumazulu (*see page 58*) in KwaZulu-Natal. Located in a prime tourism area – between the Kruger National Park and the Blyde River Canyon – it is very much part of the tourist circuit. The village features the life and traditions of the Shangaan people, its focus the bustling Marula market, where local people buy and sell produce and crafts. There is, however, much more to see that is regarded as far more 'authentic' here than at similar (and sometimes very contrived) living museums elsewhere. Shangana is located 5 km from Hazyview off the R535 towards Graskop .

Into the mainstream

Esther Mahlangu is an outstanding example of a traditional artist who has achieved enormous acclaim in the art mainstream. Mahlangu was born on a farm near Middelburg in 1935. Her mother taught her the techniques of mural painting that adorn Ndebele homesteads. Between 1980 and 1991 she was a resident of the Botshabelo Traditional Village, an open-air museum near Middelburg where she impressed visitors with her skills. In the late 1980s she visited Paris and was launched on an international career, painting a range of objects in vivid geometric designs, including a Mercedes Benz and the tailfin of a British Airways jet.

Another artist who entered the international mainstream is ceramic artist Bonnie Ntshalintshali from the Ardmore Studio. Initially regarded interesting artwork, Ardmore products are now in major galleries, collections and museums in South Africa and abroad. For links to South African art producers, a number of whom are now very highly regarded in the art word, visit www.ananzi.co.za/catalog/ArtsandCulture/ArtsandCrafts/

The customs and traditions of the Shangaan people of southern Africa play a vital role in the cultural milieu of Mpumalanga. For some insight into this ancient culture, make a point of visiting the fascinating **Shangana Cultural Village**, *(013) 737 7000, www.shangana.co.za*

One of the most attractive of such sites is the beautifully decorated Ndebele cultural village on the historic **Botshabelo** mission property a few kilometres to the north of Middelburg. There are also **Kgodwana**, a reconstruction of colourful Ndebele dwellings, with craft displays, at Kwa Mhlanga off the N4 (take the Ekandastria offramp); the village at Sudwala Caves (oddly, located at the dinosaur park), and **Matsulu** (tribal dancing, traditional food) off the N4, 40 km from Nelspruit on the way to Malelane. Next door is the **Silulu Arts and Culture Centre**. The Langeloop village, further from the main road, is a little more difficult to find: take the road towards Jeppe's Reef on the Swaziland border from the N4; turn left (before reaching Jeppe's Reef) into KwaMhluswa and right at Shonkwane. Carry on straight to the Lomati Library, where you will find **Langeloop**. Both Matsulu and Langeloop are special community development projects; at the time of writing, camp sites were being developed.

Just beyond Jeppe's Reef, over the Swaziland border, is the **Matsamo Cultural Village** (Swazi), which could be visited as part of a tour of the various Lowveld sites mentioned above. For true, traditional Swazi-style accommodation try the Ekulindeni village (and Ebutsini Lodge), which is close both to the Swaziland border and the Songimvelo Game Reserve. On offer – apart from the now almost obligatory evening dance show – there are game drives, 4x4 trails, and walks around a medicinal nursery used by traditional healers.

THE VISUAL ARTS

It was on a hillside near Revolver Creek, between Barberton and Kaapmuiden, that **Nukain Mabusa**, a Mozambican immigrant, spent 15 years creating a stone garden, applying colourful, geometric patterns to rocks he positioned across the slopes. Mabusa died in 1981, and the paint faded and the grasses covered the art. There is now an effort to preserve his work. The site is a national monument.

John Maizel's *Raw Creation: Outsider Art and Beyond* recognised Mabusa's art as one of the 44 most significant examples of such outsider art internationally (with Helen Martins; *see page 50–51*). Nelspruit's provincial legislature building incorporates a tribute to Mabusa, a monument covered in tiles enlivened by patterns inspired by his designs.

Gerard Sekoto was born at the German Lutheran mission at Botshabelo in 1913, and spent his formative years in the area, but he is perhaps better known for his connections to Johannesburg's Sophiatown. Sekota left for Paris in 1947, never to return, but his art continued to evoke memories of his life in South Africa.

A number of art galleries are clustered in and around Nelsruit, and in smaller provincial centres where communities of artists have settled (for example, in White River, Graskop, Pilgrim's Rest, Kaapschehoop and Dullstroom).

For an eye-catching example of public art, visit the legislature buildings in Nelspruit, which feature an 8-m-high, 28-panelled, embroidered and beaded wall-hanging commissioned from and produced by a group of 60 skilled rural women.

The tale of two anthems

Since 1996, South Africa has had a hybrid anthem that combines verses from the hymn and ANC anthem, *Nkosi Sikelel' I Afrika* (God Bless Africa), with parts of the pre-1994 national anthem *Die Stem van Suid Afrika* (The Call of South Africa). *Die Stem* was composed by CJ Langenhoven, who was born in the Hoeko Valley about 15 km east of Ladismith in the Western Cape. It was written in 1918 as a poem and sung for the first time in 1928, and was made the official South African anthem in 1957. *Nkosi Sikelel' I Afrika* was composed by Enoch Sontonga, who was trained at the Lovedale Institute in the Eastern Cape and taught at a Methodist missionary school in Johannesburg. Sontonga died in 1935 at the age of 32 and is buried in Johannesburg's Braamfontein Cemetery (Plot 4885). In 1996, he posthumously received the Order of Meritorious Service from President Nelson Mandela. Sontonga wrote the words – a prayer for peace and hope – in 1897 and in 1899 *Nkosi Sikelel' I Afrika* was first played in a small church. The hymn soon became popular and in 1923 it was recorded by writer and politician Sol Plaatje, followed in 1925 by its adoption as the ANC anthem. On independence, a number of African countries – Zimbabwe, Tanzania, Zambia and Namibia – customised versions as their own national anthems, some time before it was incorporated as part of South Africa's official anthem.

THEATRE

Mpumalanga's surprise is the **Casterbridge Barnyard Theatre** on the farm Casterbridge near White River, not far from the Kruger Park's Numbi Gate. Once a simple farmhouse, Casterbridge now boasts designer shops, art galleries, a cinema nouveau, and the theatre itself.

SOUNDS OF MUSIC

Mpumalanga, home to popular musician **Ray Phiri**, offers a good number of informal township jazz venues. Fred Mkhabela, who runs Middelburg's Martiq-Bonisa Ubuhle Guesthouse, organises tours to some of them. In April each year Nelspruit hosts the **Jazz in Mpumalanga Festival**, sponsored through the Standard Bank Joy of Jazz.

THE PRINTED WORD

Sir Percy Fitzpatrick's classic novel *Jock of the Bushveld* was set in the lowlands of picturesque Mpumalanga – specifically in the White River area and the southern parts of the Kruger National Park. The tale tells the story of a faithful and courageous dog, and of the couple's many adventures along the old transport route to Delagoa Bay (now known as Maputo) in Mozambique in the latter part of the 19th century.

By 1892 the route had fallen into disuse and was gradually taken back by the bushveld, but in 1950s the old (Transvaal) provincial council attached circular bronze plaques, each bearing an image of Jock, to cairns and rocks along the abandoned track. There are now Jock waymarks located near the settlements of Graskop, Sabie, White River and Klipkopje, and in the Kruger National Park near the Numbi Gate, Pretoriuskop camp, Afsaal, Phalamanzi, and Crocodile Drift on the southern border. The 'Jock' route is described in some detail in a booklet by BP Simmons entitled *In Fitzpatrick's Footsteps: Through the Present White River District* (the booklet is available at the information centre at the White River Museum).

The old mining town of **Barberton** boasts a statue of the trusty Jock. The place is also associated with the popular novelist **Bryce Courteney**, who grew up in the town (he now lives in Australia). Courteney's first bestseller, *The Power of One*, was set in the area, although travellers should be advised that not all places mentioned in the book are real. The town gaol, which features in the story, still stands, but Crystal Cave is pure fiction.

ARCHITECTURE

The province's early mining towns are interesting for their colonial architecture. **Pilgrim's Rest**, high on the escarpment, began life in the early 1870s after gold was found in the local stream and in 1974 the entire village was restored and designated a museum and a national monument. It provides an excellent example of the simple architecture of the much-romanticised late-19th-century gold-rush towns. **Barberton** is far larger in size and is still a busy urban centre (although far more sedate than in the heady gold-mining days). Many of the mining-era buildings survive and can be visited as part of the town's Heritage Trail, a self-guided walking tour.

Of the region's contemporary buildings the most significant is the provincial legislature in Nelspruit. Located above the attractive Lowveld Botanical Garden, it's an unusual, thoughtfully designed structure drawing on African idioms (the traditional village meeting place, for example) and also on classical idioms such as the Greek temple. The African-style mosaic flooring is especially beautiful.

MAKING CONTACT

White River
Museum
www.lowveldinfo.com
Pilgrim's Rest
Tourism Office
(013) 768 1060,
www.pilgrimsrest.com;
Barberton
Heritage Trail
(013) 712 2121,
barinfo@corpdial.co.za

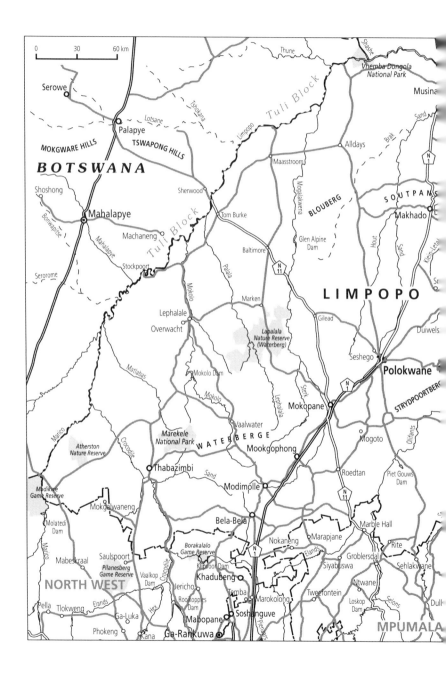

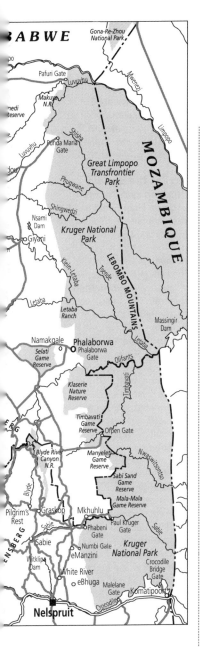

LIMPOPO

The Limpopo province, surprisingly, is home to one of the country's most vibrant and spectacular artistic traditions, that of the VhaVenda people. In recent years, the culture and its traditions have been rediscovered and individuals such as Jackson Hlungwani, Noria Mabasa, and Albert Munyai are now accepted among the leading artists in South Africa. The province also has close associations with colonial writers such as John Buchan, H Rider Haggard and the Afrikaans author and philosopher Eugene Marais.

MAKING CONTACT

**Entabeni Private
Game Reserve**
(Legend Lodges)
*(014) 743 6000, www.
legendlodges.co.za,
www.entabeni.co.za;*
**Soutpansberg
Tourism Office**
*(015) 516 0040,
www.tourism
soutpansberg.co.za;*
Mukondeni Gallery
*(011) 708 2116,
www.mukondeni.com;*
Leshaba
*(015) 593 0076,
magic@leshaba.co.za,
www.leshaba.co.za;*
Polokwane Art Museum
*(Danie Hough
Cultural Centre)*
(015) 290 2177;
**Hugh Exton
Photographic Museum**
(015) 290 2180

AFRICAN HERITAGE

The province of Limpopo (formerly known as the Northern Province) embraces several indigenous cultures, largest of which are the Pedi (or North Sotho), the VhaVenda and the Shangaan. The Pedi and Shangaan have been introduced under North West (*see page 113*) and Mpumalanga (*see page 100*).

Unique to the province are the VhaVenda, who live in and around the Soutpansberg mountains in the far north. The VhaVenda are related to the Shona people of Zimbabwe – who, in turn, are related to inhabitants of the ancient kingdoms of Great Zimbabwe and Mapungubwe.

Despite this diversity, the province has surprisingly few cultural villages of the 'living museum' kind. There is, however, a traditional Pedi hub, the big-five Entabeni private game reserve in the Waterberg mountains. Accommodation within the reserve is in the luxurious Legend lodges. For further information on cultural tours and cultural experiences in the Venda region, contact Soutpansberg tourism.

THE VISUAL ARTS

The VhaVenda artists are known mainly for allegorical carvings that incorporate traditional religious motifs, wood sculptures that are now part of art collections around South Africa, among them those of the Johannesburg Art Gallery (JAG), the South African National Gallery in Cape Town, the Pretoria Art Museum, the Tatham Gallery in Pietermaritzburg, and Nelson Mandela Metropole Art Museum in Port Elizabeth. VhaVenda carvings are also displayed and marketed at the Mukondeni Gallery, 36 Orleans Road in the suburb of Kya Sands, Johannesburg. They are also on view at their places of origin.

Art for the people

Eccentric 'outside artist' **Jackson Hlungwani** can be seen at work at the village of Mbhokota, near the Elim mission station, while **Albert Munyai** plies his trade in the village of Motale. The sculptures of **Noria Mabasa** decorate the 'Venda village' on the farm Leshaba in the Soutpansberg area. In 1995 the new owners of the farm, John and Gill Rosmarin, decided to rebuild a ruined traditional village as a visitors' retreat, and commissioned Mabasa to produce an extraordinary art tableau using VhaVenda motifs.

The province's largest formal collection is on view in the **Polokwane Art Museum's** Danie Hough Cultural Centre (at the corner of Jorissen and Schoeman streets), which has a smallish but significant collection – something over 1 000 works, which are rotated periodically. There are also a number of sculptures on permanent display in the City Plaza, and an 'industrial art park', believed to be the only one of its kind in Africa. Directly off the Plaza is the Hugh Exton Photographic Museum.

A NEW JERUSALEM

Jackson Hlungwani is an eccentric 'outside artist', his most striking claim to fame the bizarre landscape of idiosyncratic religious art – a mix of traditional and Christian symbols – he has created on the remains of a hill-top Iron Age settlement near the Limpopo village of Mbhokota.

Now in his 80s, Hlungwani is a whimsical figure. Diminutive in size, he sports long dreadlocks and wears old and fraying clothes. His birth date remains unknown but is probably around 1923. He grew up in the rural village of Nkanyani, where he herded cattle and learned to carve and work with iron. For a short while he laboured in Johannesburg, but he was injured in an industrial accident and returned to rural Limpopo, this time to Mbhokota, near Elim. In 1946 he was ordained as a priest in the Zion Christian Church (ZCC) but soon broke away to form his own congregation, known as *Yeso Galeliyo One Aposto in Sayoni Alt and Omega*. To his followers he became known as Xidonkani, or Little Donkey, a reference to the donkey who brought the pregnant Virgin Mary to Bethlehem.

The vision

Shortly after forming his church, Hlungwani began his remarkable project – the invention of a strange religious world on the summit of an acropolis-like hill near Mbhokota. For more than 30 years he added to and embellished the ruins of the ancient Age settlement, extending the dry-packed walls to create a labyrinth of passages and shrines, a strange place which he termed the New Jerusalem.

In 1978, Hlungwani had a terrifying vision that changed his life and his art. In the vision, the devil appeared to him and shot an arrow through his legs, leaving him wounded and in great agony. In the morning his legs were covered in pus- and blood-filled sores. The pain was so intense that he thought of committing suicide, but Jesus, and two other figures, appeared to him and told him that he would be healed but that he must serve God for all his life. Inspired by the dream, Hlungwani was filled with great energy and purpose, and over the next few years he produced the remarkable treasure-house of strange religious sculpture that adorns the walls of his New Jerusalem.

Carvings on view

Hlungwani was 'discovered' by the Johannesburg art world in the 1980s and quickly achieved local celebrity status. However, the commercial value and popularity of his art has resulted in the removal of almost all his sculpture from his New Jerusalem, and today the stone walls of the acropolis are bare.

In the late 1980s Hlungwani was told by God to return to the site of his father's village and rebuild it. He has named the place 'New Canaan' (a 'woman's Church', he says, in contrast to New Jerusalem, which is a 'men's Church'). However New Canaan had, at the time of writing, not progressed very far.

The artist's New Jerusalem sculptures may be seen in the Jackson Hlungwani Room in the Johannesburg Art Gallery. Among the carvings is *Tiger Fish III*, which is now the official JAG emblem.

limpopo

THEATRE

Generally speaking, the province of Limpopo doesn't really have much in the way of high-profile performing arts venues, although there are currently discussions about creating suitable facilities that will cater specifically for this cultural genre. There is, however, a small **Barnyard Theatre** situated at Stanford Lake College, Magoebaskloof.

EVENTS

Cultural events, although not nearly as prolific as they are in the larger provinces, nevertheless are an important part of the local calendar. The small village of **Haenertsburg**, which is tucked away in the mountains and woodlands near the town of Tzaneen, has developed an attractively arty feel. The community of artists who have settled in this beautiful area host at least two festivals during the year: the Haenertsburg Autumn Music, Art and Cultural Fair (a total of five days of celebration during April/May), as well as the Haenertsburg Spring Festival and Craft Fair towards the end of September. For more information on these two events, as well as other local activities, be sure to contact Magoebaskloof Tourism.

The **Oppikoppi** music festival, once held in Pretoria, has now returned to its original venue at Northam on the border between Limpopo and North West. It had rather wild beginnings in 1995, and residents around the Pretoria venue at Fountains complained about the noise – while the music lovers preferred to return to the bushveld venue anyway!

MAKING CONTACT

Barnyard Theatre
082 891 8103,
www.barnyardtheatre.co.za;
Magoebaskloof
Tourism
(015) 276 4972

THE PRINTED WORD

The misty mountains, dense forests, and ancient legends of the region provided fine material for Victorian writers in search of a raw and romantic Africa. It is likely, for example, that the mythical African Queen in **H Rider Haggard**'s *She* (1887) was based on the real-life Rain Queen of Ga-Modjadji (see also the companion volume *South Africa's Top Sites – Spiritual*).

John Buchan, author of *Prester John*, was inspired by his time spent in the Magoebaskloof and the Great Letaba valley. A memorial to John Buchan overlooks the Ebenezer Dam, approximately 5 km down the George's Valley road from Haenertsburg. Buchan, later first Baron Tweedsmuir of Elsfield, was brought to South Africa by Lord Milner shortly after the Anglo-Boer War to help with the resettlement of displaced Boers. In later years he was a distinguished British statesman and member of the British parliament, as well as the governor-general of Canada. He wrote more than 50 books during his lifetime.

Ants and baboons

The Waterberg region in the southwest of the province is linked to the writer, poet, naturalist and philosopher **Eugene Marais**, who moved to the area in a state of depression, after the Anglo-Boer War in 1903. Here he lived in close proximity to the wild chacma baboons, studied their habits and drew parallels with human beings, whom he believed were closely related. These observations were detailed in *My Friends the Baboons* (1939), *The Soul of the Ape*, which was published posthumously and in unfinished form in 1969.

He also wrote *The Soul of the White Ant*, published in 1937, shortly after his death. Sadly, after 1926, Marais was largely incapacitated by ill-health and an addiction to morphine. In March 1936 he committed suicide. There is a Eugene Marais Museum on the Entabeni Private Game Reserve (*see page*

108). For accommodation on a farm where Marais spent time writing and researching, contact Pure Palala Farmstay. Limpopo is also associated with at least three other well-known local writers. **William Plomer** and **Es'kia Mphahlele** were both born near Polokwane, while poet and critic **Njabulo Ndebele** was vice-chancellor of the University of the North near Polokwane before taking up his current (2004) position as the vice-chancellor of the University of Cape Town.

AND WHAT'S MORE...

Venture into the fascinating world of Eugene Marais. His intriguing story is showcased in the **Eugene Marais Museum** *on the Entabeni Private Game Reserve,* *(014) 743 6000,* *www.legendlodges.co.za,* *www.entabeni.co.za,* *but there are a number of other spots associated with the philosopher and poet, most notably the* **Pure Palala Farmstay** *(039) 316 6871,* *farmstay@venturenet.co.za*

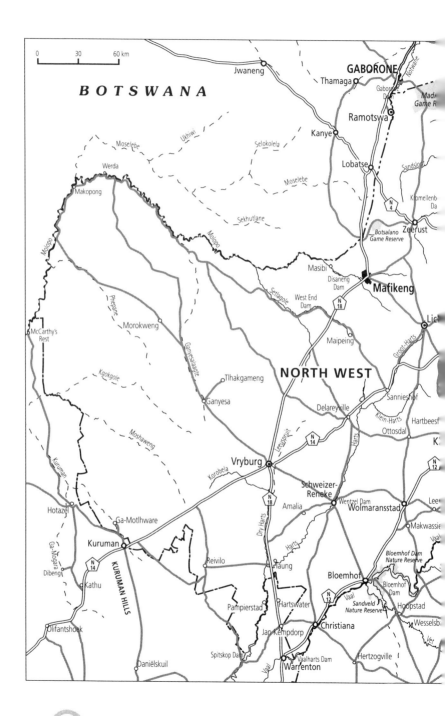

NORTH WEST

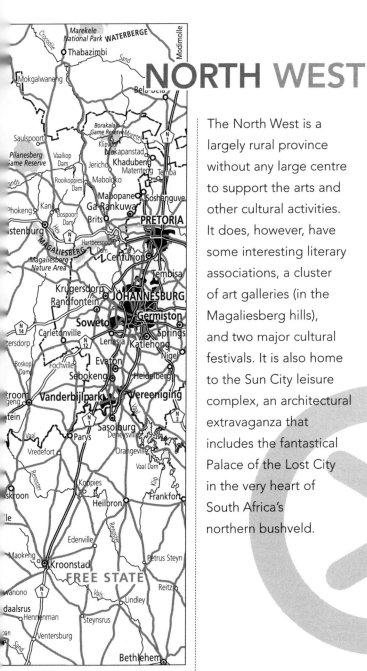

The North West is a
largely rural province
without any large centre
to support the arts and
other cultural activities.
It does, however, have
some interesting literary
associations, a cluster
of art galleries (in the
Magaliesberg hills),
and two major cultural
festivals. It is also home
to the Sun City leisure
complex, an architectural
extravaganza that
includes the fantastical
Palace of the Lost City
in the very heart of
South Africa's
northern bushveld.

AFRICAN HERITAGE

The dominant culture in North West is SeTswana although there are significant Pedi, Ndebele, and Sotho groups (and, also, traditional Afrikaner communities).

The Tswana people arrived in the region about AD1300 and gradually coalesced into major clans such as the Bangwato, Bakwena, Baralong, and Batlaping. They were devastated by the wars and great forced migrations of what is known as the *difaqane* in the early 19th century, but gradually re-established themselves. Although Botswana is a mainly SeTswana-speaking country, just as many Tswana-speakers live across the border in South Africa to the south. During the apartheid years they were considered citizens of the 'republic' of Bophuthatswana. The Sotho people are broadly related to the Tswana (who are, in fact, sometimes known as Western Sotho) as are the Pedi, or Northern Sotho. These groups speak dialects of a common language. The Ndebele, however, share many traditional beliefs and practices with the Zulu with whom they probably share a common ancestry. The Ndebele are famed for the intricate and colourful patterns that decorate the walls of their houses.

Each of these African cultures (as well as cultures from outside the region) are represented in local traditional villages. North West is home to multicultural **Lesedi**, South Africa's largest and most popular cultural village, which is located along the R512 to the north of Johannesburg on the slopes of the Magaliesberg hills.

Cultural hubs

Lesedi (which may be translated to mean 'place of light' in Sotho) is a cluster of five traditional villages that represent the architecture and practices of the Zulu, Pedi, Ndebele, Sotho, and Xhosa peoples. Visitors are housed in the decoratively traditional style (though in fact it's in three-star accommodation laid on by the Protea Hotel group) and on arrival are welcomed with song, dance and entertainment. The cultural experience continues late into the night in the bushveld *boma* (enclosure) and in the Lesedi theatre. The village is famous for its *monati* (lunch) and for its evening *nyama choma*, which has been billed as 'the biggest dance and feast show in Africa'. This is a large complex with a popular following and that features on the major tourist circuit.

There are, however, a number of other cultural villages in the province of North West.

More traditionally oriented is the **Mapoch** venue near Brits, known for the beautifully painted Ndebele dwellings and the beaded handwork of the Ndebele women (for sale at the village).

The **Gaabo Motho** cultural village is superbly situated on a mountain-top near Hebron. It features Zulu, Ndebele, Venda and Tswana cultural life, and provides a rather fascinating introduction to traditional birthing and healing practices. There is a traditional healer on site; accommodation is in Western- and traditional-style

MAKING CONTACT

Lesedi
*(012) 205 1394,
www.lesedi.com;*
Mapoch
072 630 1764;
Gaabo Motho
(012) 706 0165;
Kortkloof
*(Groot Marico
Information Office)
(014) 503 0085,
083 272 2958,*

guesthouses. There's also a small Zulu settlement known as **Buya Zulu**, which is rather oddly placed in North West, and consists of six traditional huts and a camping site for visitors to the area. Near Groot Marico is the little Tswana community of **Kortkloof** (best known for its fine traditional food and the donkey rides on offer).

The **Groot Marico** district is, of course, also a bastion of traditional Afrikaner culture, brought to endearing life in the tales of Herman Charles Bosman (*see page 116–117*), and many of the customs and traditional practices have survived the years, most famously the distilling of *mampoer* (moonshine). For further information on both Kortkloof and on the local Afrikaner community, contact Groot Marico Information.

For a further experience of Afrikaner pioneer lifestyle visit the Ring Wagon Inn situated close to Hartbeestpoort Dam. Here visitors are accommodated in a traditional *laager* (or circle of wagons) and are treated to authentic *boerekos* (Afrikaner cuisine) and, naturally, the obligatory *mampoer*.

THE VISUAL ARTS
The mountains of the Magaliesberg are an easy day's outing from both Pretoria and Johannesburg, and have attracted a cluster of art galleries, studios and workshops. These imaginative venues form a large part of the increasingly popular initiative

known as the **Magalies Meander**, an entertaining and rewarding touring route that is seeing more and more visitors every year.

Art galleries that feature on the Magalies Meander include Adante Art, Adou Art, Angela Eidelman, the Barn Gallery, Dietmar Weining, Jo Roos, and Kosmos Art. There is also a large cluster of arts-and-craft shops at Chameleon Village.

North West has links with **Irma Stern**, one of the country's most respected artists: she was born in the village of Schweizer-Reneke, to a wealthy German-Jewish family. The province also has its own 'outsider artist', the eccentric **Elias Molefe**, who has developed his fantasy garden on the outskirts of the Sun City complex. Molefe uses his art, constructed from household refuse, to teach the lessons of life – lessons about sex and HIV/Aids, drinking and driving, child abuse, and war.

THE PERFORMING ARTS
A number of towns in the province have civic or theatre halls, but the most glamorous venue is the **Sun City Theatre** in Sol Kerzner's fantasy land on the edge of the Pilanesberg. The theatre plays host to glittering extravaganzas and floor shows. With its four luxury hotels and the Palace of the Lost City, Sun City sits adjacent to the Big Five Pilanesberg Game Reserve in an ancient volcanic complex. The resort boasts more than 25 000 visitors a day and remains a major attraction of the area.

The **Aardklop Nasionale Kunstefees**, which is held in Potchefstroom each September, is an Afrikaans cultural festival that was once described as the 'thinking modern Boer's arty party'. Although hosted by a town known for a particularly austere brand of Afrikaner conservatism, the festival is rapidly growing in popularity and has come to symbolise the reinvention of the 'new' Afrikaner culture. Among the many leading performers appearing at the event have been rock artists such as Karen Zoid and Amanda Strijdom, but by 2003 a number of black musicians and bands (including such greats Dolly Rathebe and the African Jazz Pioneers) were major players.

The world of Herman Charles Bosman

The Groot Marico is a familiar name to a generation of South Africans who grew up reading the tales of Herman Charles Bosman and who watched them dramatised by the popular actor, Patrick Mynhardt.

In the 1920s Bosman was a teacher in the Groot Marico District, at a small farm school in the village of Nietverdiend, close to the present-day Madikwe game reserve. He was to stay in the area for just six months, but this was enough to provide the material for his bushveld stories. His stay was cut short by a dramatic event: over the July school holiday in 1926, he killed his step-brother during an argument and was placed on death row in the Johannesburg Fort. His sentence was commuted, however, and he was released after four years. At the time of writing (2004) the farm school, which had closed in 1938, was in ruins, and had become the centre of a media controversy after entry to the site had been barred by a new landowner.

Tales from the *voorkamer*

Bosman's stories capture the spirit of the 'backveld', and especially of the rural and isolated Afrikaner community. The sometimes unflattering image he presents of the Marico Boers as backward and troublesome is counterbalanced by an appreciation of their unrefined wisdom. The humour is satirical but also compassionate.

The setting for the stories, published in collections such as *Mafeking Road*, *In the Withaaks Shade*, *Unto Dust*, and *A Bekkersdal Marathon*, is usually Jurie Steyn's *voorkamer* (front room), where five or so residents meet each week to drink coffee, smoke their pipes and await the arrival of the postal lorry. They are odd collection indeed: the inimitable Oom Schalk Lourens, the story-teller; Gysbert van Tonder, part-time cattle-smuggler; Chris Welman; Johnnie Coen; and Oupa Sarel Bekker. The enchanting stories dwell on the daily lives of the Marico community, on drought, the rinderpest, *miltsiekte*, ('milk sickness', or anthrax), cattle smuggling, and friends and neighbours who have disappeared into the iniquitous city of Johannesburg.

THE PRINTED PAGE

The North West province is strongly identified with the legacy of writer **Herman Charles Bosman**, who lived for a while in the region, and who based his widely popular 'bushveld tales' on his own experiences in a typical rural Afrikaner community in the Groot Marico district (*see below*).

The province is also associated with the African writer and politician **Sol Plaatje** (see the companion volume *South Africa's Top Sites – Struggle*). Before the Anglo-Boer War, Plaatje served in Mafikeng as a court interpreter, and lived at Silas Morema's house 'Maratiwa', and during the siege itself as well as its aftermath he worked as a war

Marico today

The little hamlet of Groot Marico gave its name to the district, and has come to be associated with Bosman, although there is no evidence that Bosman ever spent time in the village. The school he attended was, in fact, some distance away.

The benefits that Groot Marico enjoys today from its association with Bosman is largely due to the vision and energies of Egbert and Santa van Bart, who manage the Groot Marico Information Centre. Egbert, with his long beard and rugged looks, is an Oom Schalk Lourens look-alike. He is also the chairperson of the Herman Charles Bosman Literary Society, which hosts the Herman Charles Bosman Festival in October each year, while his wife Santa is a social worker who has run a community arts project (the initiative has a retail outlet at the information centre) that has provided income for poor families in the district.

This couple has made a huge impact in the district. During the great drought of the 1980s, for example, they persuaded farmers in this marginal agricultural district to turn from cattle farming to tourism and game farming and, in doing so, helped protect the ecologically threatened bushveld as well as a create new source of income for many households.

The Groot Marico is a small but highly diverse community. There is a traditional, conservative Afrikaner farming community that settled in the district about 150 years ago, and whose names echo in the pages of the Bosman stories. There is also an influential Muslim group that has lived and traded in the village since 1906 (despite apartheid restrictions), and a black community that is still extremely poor and marginalised. Surprisingly, the village is also home to a growing number of writers, artists, and practitioners of alternative healing, who occasionally clash with the more conservative elements in the area. Groot Marico is a place of surprises – it has a compelling landscape, fascinating characters, deep ironies. It must rate as one of South Africa's top destinations for the 'literary traveller'.

AND WHAT'S MORE...

The Groot Marico district is a delight for those intent on meeting the eccentric characters of the world of Herman Charles Bosman. While life here may not be quite as romantic as the famed author would have us believe, it is nevertheless an intriguing place. For information on attractions and accommodation, contact the Van Barts at the **Groot Marico Information Centre** *(014) 503 0085, 083 272 2958, info@marico.co.za, www.marico.co.za*

correspondent and later wrote *Mafeking Diary: A Black Man's View of a White Man's War*. He also set up a printing press and office on the town's Shippard Street (which can still be seen) and launched the first Setswana newspaper, *Koranta ea Becoana*, before moving to larger premises on the corner of Warren and Main Streets.

During this time Plaatje occupied a house off Bray Road in Ramosadi Village on the edge of town. The ruins of the house are still visible; from the Vryburg road from Mafikeng turn right into Bray Road towards the airport; turn off the road a few hundred metres on the left, where the Plaatje house is signposted, and pass through a rusty gate at an abandoned store. The ruins are on your left. In 1909 Plaatje's newspaper ceased publication and he moved, debt-ridden, to Kimberley, where his career finally took off.

The treasures of ancient civilisations

South Africa may lack the treasures of the great ancient civilisations boasted by regions such as Egypt or Mesopotamia (Iraq), but it does have some extraordinary artwork linked to African kingdoms that date back more than 1 000 years. South Africa's very own 'lost city of gold' is **Mapungubwe** in Limpopo Province (see companion volume *South Africa's Top Sites – Science*).

The people of Mapungubwe were part of a vast trading network that extended to the Far East and included the exchange of valuables such as gold, copper, ivory and animal skins. Over 20 graves have been excavated at the Mapungubwe site and many of these have yielded art treasures, including a gold rhinoceros, a golden sceptre and a gold bowl. These treasures may be seen in the Mapungubwe Collection at the University of Pretoria.

Significant art treasures have also recently been uncovered at the **Thulamela** site in the far north of the Kruger National Park, where numerous gold beads and bangles were unearthed during excavations of the site.

An excellent display of Africa's gold artefacts is to be found in the newly opened **Gold of Africa Museum** in Martin Melck House at 96 Strand Street, Cape Town, which has the world's largest collection of artefacts from Africa's gold-rich civilisations. The collection was put together by a Swiss art lover and is now under the custodianship of the gold-mining giant, Anglo-Gold Ashanti.

Although gold is probably the most romantic of the metals, iron and copper artefacts are often equally significant and of considerable interest to visitors to these ancient sites. There have been very important finds of such artefacts in places such as **Phalaborwa** in Limpopo Province and **Molokwane** in North West (see the companion volume *South Africa's Top Sites – Science*).

MAKING CONTACT

Maratiwa
(018) 381 6102;
Groot Marico
Information Centre
(014) 503 0085,
083 272 2958,
info@marico.co.za,
www.marico.co.za;
Magalies Meander
(014) 577 1733/1845, www.
magaliesmeander.co.za;
Magaliesberg Information
www.magaliesinfo.co.za;
Mapungubwe Collection
(University of Pretoria)
(012) 420 3146, www.
mapungubwe.up.ac.za;
Gold of Africa Museum
(Martin Melck House)
(021) 405 1540

ARCHITECTURE

The traditional Ndebele style of domestic architecture, striking in its geometrical patterns and bright colours decoration, can be seen here and there but probably at its best at the Mapoch Ndebele 'living museum' 2 km from the Marula Sun casino, near Brits. It's an exuberant idiom that stands in sharp contrast to the generally dreary modern buildings of most of the province's towns.

The major architectural monument to HF Verwoerd's segregationist vision is **Mmabatho**, capital of the erstwhile 'republic' of Bophuthatswana. In line with the regime's 'grand apartheid' schemes for what was called regional 'independence', the new capital was designed on a grand scale – government offices, university, convention centre, large airport, independence stadium. As with so many 'planned towns', though, there is simply too much space, and the place seems sterile when compared with busy, shabby Mafikeng next door.

Then there's the huge **Sun City** hotel, casino and leisure complex close to the Pilanesberg mountains to the north of Rustenburg. This great kingdom of pleasure, on the edge of an ancient volcano, was built by Sol Kerzner and his Sun International enterprise in the aforesaid 'independent' country of Bophuthatswana, as gambling and other forms of adult entertainment were then prohibited in 'white' South Africa. This is post-Modern fantasy on a truly monumental scale; even H Rider Haggard would have been astonished at the bizarre reconstruction of a mythical African landscape in this otherwise harsh landscape. The complex embraces four hotels (including the ultra-plush Palace of the Lost City), a massive entertainment centre and casino, two world-class golf courses, a 25-ha jungle with over 3 500 planted trees, and the Valley of the Waves with its golden beaches and artificially created rollers.

AND WHAT'S MORE...

Never let it be said that South Africa is not a land of fascinating contrasts. While examples of the unique diversity of both the country's people and its landscape lay scattered across the land, nowhere is this contrast as obvious as it is in North West – where places that are worlds apart sit shoulder to shoulder on the harsh veld. To experience this land of extremes, make a point of visiting the cultural village of **Mapoch** *(012) 706 0102, which showcases the traditional homesteads of the Ndebele people, and then – for a real culture shock – see the opulent African-Baroque of the mammoth* **Sun City Complex** *(014) 557 1000, www.suncity.co.za, www.suninternational.co.za*

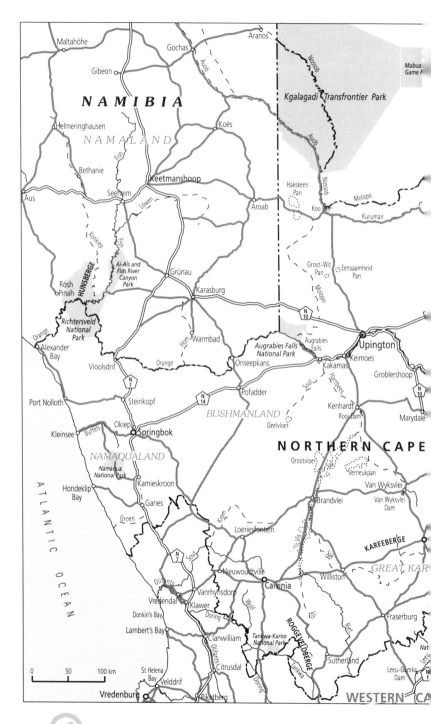

Maltahöhe

Gochas

Aranos

Mabua
Game P

Gibeon

NAMIBIA

Kgalagadi Transfrontier Park

Nossob

Helmeringhausen

Koës

NAMALAND

Auob

Fish

Bethanie

Keetmanshoop

Hakskeen
Pan

Nossob

Seeheim

Molopo

Aus

Löwen

Aroab

Koo Pan

Kuruman

Konkiep

Fish

Groot-Wit
Pan

Eensaamheid
Pan

Ai-Ais and
Fish River
Canyon
Park

Grünau

HUNSBERGE

Rosh
Pinah

Karasburg

Molopo

Richtersveld
National
Park

Orange

Hom

Warmbad

Augrabies Falls
National Park

Augrabies
Falls

N
10

Upington

Alexander
Bay

Vioolsdrif

Orange

Onseepkans

Kakamas

Keimoes

Groblershoop

N
7

Sout

Hartbees

N
10

Port Nolloth

Steinkopf

N
14

Pofadder

Kenhardt

Kleinsee

Buffels

Okiep

Springbok

BUSHMANLAND

Geelvloer

Rooidam

Marydale

NAMAQUALAND

Grootvloer

NORTHERN CAPE

Namaqua
National Park

Kamieskroon

Verneukpan

Hondeklip
Bay

Garies

Brandvlei

Van Wyksvlei

Van Wyksvlei
Dam

A T L A N T I C

Groen

Kougm

Loeriesfontein

Vis

Sak

KAREEBERGE

N
7

Sout

Nieuwoudtville

Williston

GREAT KAR

O C E A N

Olifants

Calvinia

Vanrhynsdorp

Vredendal

Klawer

Doring

Wolf

Vis

Riet

Fraserburg

Donkin's Bay

ROGGEVELDBERGE

Lambert's Bay

Clanwilliam

Tankwa-Karoo
National Park

Sutherland

Nat

Olifants

0   50   100 km

St Helena
Bay

Velddrif

Citrusdal

Doring

Tankwa

Leeu

Leeu-Gamka
Dam

N
1

Vredenburg

Pikerberg

WESTERN CA

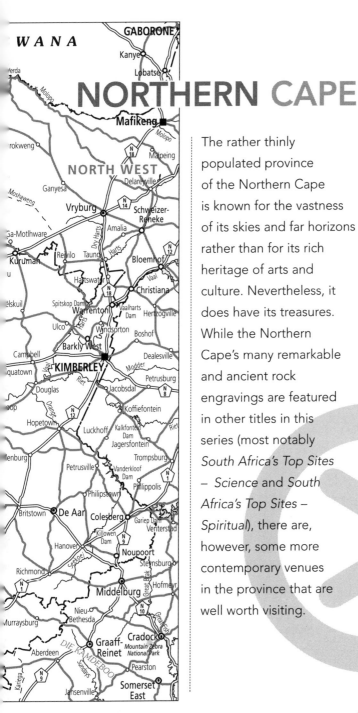

NORTHERN CAPE

The rather thinly populated province of the Northern Cape is known for the vastness of its skies and far horizons rather than for its rich heritage of arts and culture. Nevertheless, it does have its treasures. While the Northern Cape's many remarkable and ancient rock engravings are featured in other titles in this series (most notably *South Africa's Top Sites – Science* and *South Africa's Top Sites – Spiritual*), there are, however, some more contemporary venues in the province that are well worth visiting.

THE VISUAL ARTS

The **William Humphreys Art Gallery**, in Kimberley's civic centre, competes with Bloemfontein's Oiliewenhuis (*see page 72*) as the country's best art museum outside the major centres. It has a good collection of Dutch, Flemish, British and French art from the 1500s and 1600s, and a growing collection of South African works that includes Moses Kottler's sculpture *Nudes* (1957) (once adjudged an affront to public morals and removed from display), Noria Mabasa's *Natal Flood Disaster* (1988), and *Tamfuti* (1988) by Bonnie Ntshalintshali from Ardmore (*see page 60*).

The museum also contains 247 European works put together in the 1930s by Reverend George Lawson, the archdeacon of the Kuruman mission, who compiled it, from catalogues, from this outpost. Also on display are linocuts from the !Xu and Khwe San Art and Craft Project (*see below*), among them a work dedicated to Ruyter, an !Xam who was beaten to death by a farmer for his faulty shepherding.

For an excellent introduction to precolonial art and artefacts, visit the **McGregor Museum** in Egerton Road, Kimberley. Next door is the **Duggan Cronin Gallery**, which exhibits the astonishing photography of Alfred Cronin.

Cronin resigned from the Jesuit priesthood and, at 23, emigrated to South Africa in 1897, and developed a passionate interest in the photography of indigenous people, beginning with labourers in De Beers' mining compounds. In 1919 he made his first expedition into the Kalahari (or Kgalagadi) to photograph the Bushman (San) and Tswana peoples, and spent the next two decades travelling more than 128 000 km, recording every major ethnic group in southern Africa.

The gallery, officially opened in 1938 by Sir Ernest Oppenheimer, was established to preserve the memory of the 'vanishing traditions of tribal people'. In 1947 the British royal family paid a visit. The gallery has seen better days but is still important.

Reviving the art of the San

One of the country's more unusual and interesting cultural projects is based on the farm Platfontein, near Kimberley. It's the site of the famous Wildebeestkuil rock engravings, and the place to which the !Xu and Khwe (these are San, or Bushman, clans) have been moved from the tent camp at Schmidtsdrif. The two displaced groups were airlifted to South Africa when Namibia gained its independence in the late 1980s, the move prompted by fear of retribution from the SWAPO government: many of the poverty-stricken Bushmen had worked as trackers for the South African Defence Force during the border war. For years afterwards they lived in dire conditions at Schmidtsdrif, and it is only very recently that they've been provided with land of their own.

Although the !Xu and Khwe now have a level of security, they are still desperately poor; and most are unemployed. It is this problem that the !Xu and Khwe San Art and Craft Project seeks to address.

MAKING CONTACT

William Humphreys
Art Gallery
(053) 831 1724/5;
McGregor Museum
(053) 839 2700;
Duggan Cronin Gallery
(053) 842 0099

THE PERFORMING ARTS

The province's biggest auditorium is the **Northern Cape Theatre** in Kimberley. However, with its dry climate, the region is extremely well suited to outdoor performances, and these are held in such venues as the Oppenheimer Gardens in Kimberley, and the Galeshewe Stadium just outside the city.

Perhaps more interesting, though, is the **Apollo Theatre** in the small Karoo town of Victoria West, which was built in Art Deco style in the 1920s and converted to a 'talkies' cinema after World War II. The theatre-cum-cinema fell into disuse during the 1970s, but was finally restored by travel writer David Robbins in the 1990s and then transformed into a multifaceted arts, cultural and community-development centre. The Apollo Film Festival, which is held in this enchanting place during September and October each year, has been described as a 'showcase of South African independent film' (for information, contact the Apollo Development Association).

The other surprise is the tiny Karoo hamlet of **Middelpos**, birthplace of the acclaimed Shakespearean actor **Anthony Sher**. This dusty and isolated outpost was in fact founded by Sher's family, which had fled persecution in Lithuania.

EVENTS

The provincial department of Sports, Arts, and Culture is working hard to promote cultural activities and has put together a programme of events through the year, among them jazz festivals and concerts. Each September Kimberley hosts the Vukani Arts and Culture Festival which, although small in comparison with other festivals in South Africa, offers an entertaining medley of jazz, choral music, gospel, Bushman dance and story-telling.

MAKING CONTACT

Northern Cape Theatre
(053) 839 2000;
Apollo Theatre
(Apollo Development Association)
(053) 621 1185,
apollotheatre@intekom.co.za,
www.apollotheatre.co.za;
Northern Cape Department of Sports, Arts and Culture
(053) 831 1761;
Vukani Arts and Culture Festival
(053) 831 4152

The project's founder, Catherine Scheepers-Meyer, launched the Kuru Art project in Botswana, among Bushman shepherds and domestic workers. Moved by the plight of the !Xu and Khwe, she sent a proposal for a job-creating scheme to the commanding officer at Schmidtsdrif, and began her work in a trailer, encouraging people to reconnect with their artistic traditions. In 1996 Scheepers-Meyer left Schmidtsdrif and handed over the project to Riette Mierke. who remains the coordinator.

The project has now been relocated to Platfontein, where a ceramics studio and pottery and textile workshops have been established. The art is marketed at Wildebeestkuil visitors' centre near the engravings. It's also been exhibited nationally and internationally, and is reproduced in Marlene Sullivan Winberg's *My Eland's Heart*. The top-selling artist was Tuoi Stefaans Samcuia, whose massive three-panel linocut decorates the foyer of the Cape Town International Convention Centre. Sadly, Samcuia died in June 2003 of tuberculosis.

AND WHAT'S MORE...

For some insight into the world of the descendants of the San, and their life experiences in latter-day South Africa, head for the **!Xu and Khwe San Art and Craft Project** *at Platfontein, where members of the community craft ceramics and textiles made available to the public at the Wildebeestkuil visitors' centre. Contact the project on (053) 833 7069, xukhwe@iafrica.com*

THE PRINTED WORD

Kimberley was home to **Sol Plaatje**, founding member of the African National Congress and the first black African to write a novel in English. The city recently honoured the memory of this celebrated South African by naming its municipal area the Sol Plaatje Local Municipality.

Plaatje was born in the village of Podisetlhogo, 80 km northeast of the Pniel Lutheran Mission near Barkly West, where he received his early education. He worked in the Kimberley postal service before moving to Mafikeng, and on returning to Kimberley, in 1909, he took up residence at 32 Angel Street, located in the (then) 'Malay Camp' near the city centre.

During his time Plaatje was appointed the first secretary-general of the ANC, and wrote his major works, *Native Life in South Africa* (1916) and *Mhudi* (1930). He was buried in Kimberley's West End cemetery in June 1932, and his grave was declared a national monument in 1998. In 1992, 32 Angel Street was purchased by the Sol Plaatje Educational Trust with funds donated by the ANC, Anglo American and De Beers. The house, now open to the public, incorporates a small museum featuring Plaatje's life, and a library and research centre devoted to black literature and the Setswana language. Visits can be arranged.

Desert tales

Kimberley is associated with the internationally recognised author **Dan Jacobson**, who spent his schooldays in the city and later set his novels – including *The Trap* (1955), *Dance in the Sun* (1957), and *The Price of Diamonds* (1957) – in the vast landscapes of the Northern Cape. The region also has some association with **Olive Schreiner** – although she was born in the Eastern Cape and spent much of her life around the town of Cradock, she did live for a time in the province. There are Olive Schreiner houses in De Aar (now functioning as a restaurant), and in Grace Street, Hanover.

Afrikaans writers connected with the Northern Cape include **Ingrid Jonker**, who challenged the conservatism of Afrikaner society in her works, and was born on a farm near Kimberley. **NP van Wyk Louw** began his life in 1906 in Sutherland; his family house is now a museum (contact the tourism office). Although Van Wyk Louw was to study and work at the University of Cape Town, and then in Amsterdam in The Netherlands, he always longed for his home town. The great sunlit expanses of the Karoo had a huge impact on his poetry.

Upington was the beginning of the heroine's odyssey in **Elsa Joubert's** moving novel, *The Long Journey of Poppie Nongena* (first published in Afrikaans in 1978 and translated into English shortly thereafter). Joubert based her novel on a woman who lived in a small house in Upington's oldest township, known initially as Blikkies and now called Progress. Many of the older residents still remember the woman who became known as Poppie. The municipality has plans to buy the house and develop it as a tourist attraction.

ARCHITECTURE

Much of the traditional architecture of the **Nama** people has disappeared, but remnants may still be seen in the Richtersveld area – in the national park and around the villages of Eksteenfontein, Khubus and Lekkersing. The Nama dwelling, known as the *matjieshuis*, is a portable, dome-shaped structure with a framework of light poles traditionally covered with grass mats, and it's well suited to cope with the scorching heat of the Northern Cape.

Interestingly, the region's early European settlers, the so-called *trekboers*, adopted a similar shape for their simple dwellings, and a few of their 18th-century corbelled houses, built of flat stones, survive near the small towns of Carnavon, Williston and Fraserburg. A particularly odd structure in Fraserburg is the tall, six-sided *peperbus*, designed and constructed by the Reverend Bamberger in 1861. The building has had chequered history, serving at various times as municipal office, post office, church, magistrate's court, and powder magazine depot.

Styles on show

The Northern Cape has also inherited an interesting legacy of **colonial mining** architecture, earliest examples of which is to be found around the small Namaqualand towns of Okiep and Springbok. Here, Cornish mine pumps and smokestacks are preserved as national monuments.

More extensive, however, is the early architecture of Kimberley, where the early mining camp has been reconstructed, around the famous Big Hole, to create an impressive open-air museum; important buildings from the period include the De Beer's head office in Stockdale Street (1888), the Kimberley Club in Du Toit's Road (1881), as well as the McGregor Museum in Atlas Street (1897).

There are also many beautiful **religious** buildings in the province, the most remarkable of them perhaps Robert Moffat's 'Cathedral of the Kalahari' (1838) at the Kuruman Mission, which was once the largest structure in the South African interior, and the glorious Catholic cathedral at Pella (1885). See also the companion volume *South Africa's Top Sites – Spiritual.*

There is relatively little to see in the way of interesting **contemporary** architecture in the province, though one notable exception is the new and avant-garde Northern Cape legislature building in Kimberley. This iconic structure is a work of art: instead of straight lines and sharp angles it is distinguished by gentle curves, and features images, mosaics, and textures that reflect the indigenous region's diverse cultures.

For **space-age** architecture see the new South African Large Telescope (SALT) building at the South African Astronomical Observatory near Sutherland. This huge complex, covered with a mirror truss and topped by a large aluminium space-frame dome, houses one of the world's biggest telescopes (see also the companion volume *South Africa's Top Sites – Science*).

MAKING CONTACT

Kimberley
Open-air Museum
(053) 833 1557;
Kuruman Mission
(053) 712 1352;
**South African
Large Telescope**
*(South African
Astronomical Observatory)*
(023) 571 1205,
www.salt.ac.za,
www.saao.ac.za

INDEX